Birthday a Day

Grades 3 and up

Stephen Currie

Acknowledgements and Dedication

My thanks to all my students and colleagues at Poughkeepsie Day School who have helped shape this book over the last five years. Thanks also go to my family (extended as well as immediate), my editor, and the staffs of several libraries, local and otherwise. And finally, I'd like to dedicate the book: to May 11, July 22, and November 21, with love.

GoodYearBooks

are available for most basic curriculum subjects plus many enrichment areas. For more GoodYearBooks, contact your local bookseller or educational dealer. For a complete catalog with information about other GoodYearBooks, please write:

GoodYearBooks
ScottForesman
1900 East Lake Avenue
Glenview, IL 60025

Introduction

Birthday a Day presents 366 short biographies of 366 people, both past and present, who have made a difference in the world. For each day of the year you will find a short biography of a famous (or not-so-famous!) person born on that day. The subjects of the biographies are drawn from all walks of life and from all over the globe. Each entry provides the year and place of the subject's birth, along with information about that person and a suggestion for a follow-up activity relating to his or her life and work.

This book is intended to be a selection of 366 short stories from history which give children a picture of how and why the world is the way it is today. I chose biographical subjects accordingly, with the intention of getting a cross-section of interesting, important, and colorful people. The people featured in this book are not intended to be a listing of the 366 most significant people who ever lived. No insult is meant to people who are "left out" of the book. There were many great and fascinating people I was sorry not to be able to include.

The information in this book is as accurate as possible. I consulted literally hundreds of sources in putting it together—and I needed them all. At times it seemed to be the exception, rather than the rule, for sources to agree on even the most basic information. Birth years are a good example. For several people, such as Mother Jones, Loretta Lynn, and Jomo Kenyatta, it's easy to find two or even three different birth years. In some cases, people made themselves out to be older or younger than they really were. In other cases, records are faulty or have been misinterpreted. I've chosen the year that I thought was based on the best available evidence. There are similar problems with birthplaces (poor record-keeping and shifting political boundaries are the main culprits here), spellings (many reference books give different versions of Carry Nation, Tenzing Norkay, and Jim Beckwourth), and even birthdays themselves. If my information conflicts with your encyclopedia's, I can only apologize, and assure you that I did my best to find the most reliable information.

How to Use This Book

While it can be fun for children to flip through the biographies at random, trading bits and pieces of information as they go, the structure of the book lends itself better to studying one person each day. On the first of May, for instance, children can read about the fiery Mother Jones and her efforts to win justice for workers in the early part of the century; the following day, they can celebrate the birthday of the little-known African-American engineer and inventor Elijah McCoy. Reading one entry a day and discussing it—however briefly—can help provide structure to a school day. Once children are used to these daily biographies, they will eagerly look forward to learning about the next "birthday person."

Besides the projects suggested for each individual entry, there are many ways of using the birthday biographies in class. Writing assignments are an obvious example. Children can use the facts of people's lives as a springboard to writing stories, short plays, or dialogues about them. Alternatively, once children have read several of these biographies, they can be asked to write about which people they think are similar, and why; which people might have liked each other, and why; or which people they would most like to have met. Essays like these can be shared with the rest of the class, often sparking interesting discussions! Children can be asked to rewrite an entry in verse, to retell a subject's life to make the story appealing to a younger child, or even to invent and write about a person born "September 31." Of course, these are just some of the many possible writing assignments based on the biographies.

Library research is another good way to make use of the biographies. More detailed biographies of many—though not all—of the subjects can be found in encyclopedias, biographical dictionaries, and other sources listed in the Suggestions for Further Reading section below. Working alone or in pairs, children can choose a person from the book, draw up a list of further information they would like to have, and prepare a written or oral report based on outside reading. Children can also research the topics discussed within the entries, such as civil rights, gospel music, or chimpanzees, among many others.

The biographies in *Birthday a Day* lend themselves to use with other parts of the curriculum as well. To develop geographical knowledge, post a map at the front of the classroom. For each new biography, children can find the country or state where the subject was born. The children in my classes always enjoy shading in the countries and states as they come up. To connect the biographies with math, have children calculate how old each birthday person is or would be if he or she were alive today. Are there any helpful patterns or shortcuts to make the computations easier? Some of the more unusual names make challenging bonus words for spelling practice, and a couple of weeks' worth of birthdays are good for alphabetizing (no fair looking in the index!) or sequencing by year of birth.

Once children are familiar with a number of the people in the book, they can play a "Twenty Questions" game to encourage logical thinking. One child thinks of a person featured in the book. To find out who it is, the other children have to ask questions with yes or no answers: "Was your person born in the United States?" or "Did your person have something to do with science?" would be good examples. Keep track of how many questions it took to figure out who the mystery person was, and talk about which questions were most helpful in narrowing down the possibilities.

Daily work with the birthday people can be as long or as short as you wish. In my classroom, I use them as a central focus. Many of our science and social studies projects spring directly from the birthday people's lives, and every day we use them for practice in writing, computation, and map skills. However, it's not necessary to go into this much detail to make good use of the book. The biographies can be used now and again as fillers for days when time seems to stretch on and on. Some teachers might prefer to read from the book as a five-minute routine each morning with only brief follow-ups; still others might choose to play up some people or projects, but not others. Any way you decide to use them, I expect your students will enjoy learning about these interesting historical figures—and you may be surprised at the depth of their understanding and recollection of their lives and times.

Suggestions for Further Reading

The *Current Biography* series gives detailed information on almost all famous people since World War II; it was one of my most useful sources. *Dictionary of American Biography* and *Cyclopedia of American Biography* include long articles on many Americans who are well-known (and the latter especially, for many who aren't); the information in some of the older volumes is not always to be trusted, however. The four-volume *Notable American Women* series is also quite valuable. *Something About the Author* does for children's book authors what *The Grove Dictionary of Music* does for classical (and some popular) musicians: both offer detailed and usually readable biographies. There are other similar volumes and series about African-American women, Asian-Americans, artists, scientists, military figures, and many others; ask your librarian. I also made some use of two encyclopedia sets *(Academic American Encyclopedia* and *Encyclopaedia Britannica)*, along with old issues of *Time, Newsweek,* and *The New York Times.*

Betsy Ross

1752, Pennsylvania

Have you ever been punished for something you didn't do? Betsy was praised for something she never did. Betsy worked with needle and thread. She made clothes, and she stuffed and sewed armchairs and mattresses. When she needed extra money, Betsy sewed flags for the state of Pennsylvania.

But she is best known for another project. Many history books say that Betsy designed the pattern of stars and stripes that became the flag of the United States. It's a great story. But it's completely false. Her grandson made it all up after Betsy died.

Design your own flag. Make it from paper or cloth.

2

Lillian Leitzel
1893, Germany

On a good day, Lillian spent a lot of time upside down.

Lillian was less than five feet tall, but she was tremendously strong. She needed to be. Lillian was a circus acrobat. Though circuses usually have three different acts going on at once, everyone else stopped when it was Lillian's turn to perform. With the spotlight on her, she climbed a rope to a ring hanging high above the floor. Then she swung her body up and around the ring, while the audience counted the spins. Her all-time record was 249. That's a lot—especially considering that she held onto the ring with only one arm!

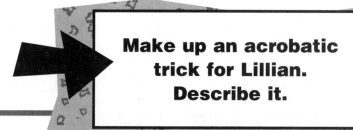

Make up an acrobatic trick for Lillian. Describe it.

From *Birthday a Day*, published by GoodYearBooks. Copyright © 1996 Stephen Currie.

January

3

Lucretia Mott
1793, Massachusetts

The Declaration of Independence says: "All men are created equal." Lucretia and a friend suggested that this line really should read, "All men and women are created equal."

Lucretia worked for women's rights. To some, "women's rights" just meant the opportunity to vote. But Lucretia wanted much more: good jobs, fair pay, the chance to go to college. Lucretia had grown up on an island where the men were usually away at sea. With no men around, the women ran things. Lucretia got used to women having power. When she grew up, she was surprised to find that this wasn't true everywhere!

What does "created equal" mean? Explain it in your own words.

Louis Braille
1809, France

If someone put a magnetic letter in your hand, could you tell what it was without looking? Maybe. But you'd probably have to feel every corner of the letter. Years ago, that was how blind children learned to read. It was slow and tricky, and making all those letters cost lots of money.

Louis changed all that. Blinded at age three, he knew there had to be a better way. So he invented one: a code of raised dots. Each arrangement of dots stood for a different letter. Blind people could read by running their fingers along the dots. Today we honor Louis by calling his code "Braille."

Cut out letters from cardboard. Feel them to tell which is which.

From *Birthday a Day*, published by GoodYearBooks. Copyright © 1996 Stephen Currie.

January

5

Shah Jahan
1592, India

Shah Jahan's name means King of the World, and he did rule quite a lot of it. When his wife Mumtaz died, Shah Jahan was brokenhearted. For two years, he thought of her constantly. Not even music could cheer him up. Still, Shah Jahan found a way to deal with his grief. He helped design an enormous building which would be Mumtaz's tomb. Made mostly of marble, it looked like a palace. Shah Jahan called his magnificent building the Taj Mahal. People traveled miles to see it—and they still do today.

Design your own palace. What will it be made of?

From *Birthday a Day*, published by GoodYearBooks. Copyright © 1996 Stephen Currie.

Joan of Arc
1412, France

Joan was a shepherdess. She lived in a part of France ruled by the English. When she was a girl, she often heard voices, which she believed came from heaven. The voices told her to drive the English out of France. Joan was no soldier, but she did what she was told. For several months she led the French army into one battle after another. Joan never fought; she planned strategy and urged the troops forward. Though she was captured and killed, the war went on till the French had won. An old story said that France would someday be saved by a girl. Apparently, it was right!

Research weapons used in France during Joan's time.

From *Birthday a Day*, published by GoodYearBooks. Copyright © 1996 Stephen Currie.

Zora Neale Hurston

1901, Florida

When Zora was thirteen, her older brother told her to quit school and take care of his children. Zora didn't like that idea, so she ran away. She put herself through high school and college, giving manicures to earn enough money.

Zora was deeply interested in people like her—African Americans in the South. After college, she went back to Florida to collect their folktales and songs. She wrote her own novels too. The most famous was called *Their Eyes Were Watching God*. Not bad for a woman who thought her eyes might only get to watch her nieces and nephews!

Name the three qualities you think a writer needs most. Explain why.

January

8

Fanny Bullock Workman

1859, Massachusetts

Fanny believed in exercise—and as much of it as possible. A century ago, when bicycles and roads weren't nearly as good as they are now, she biked fifty miles every day. But Fanny liked mountains best. She traveled to Europe, Asia, and North America. Wherever she went, she climbed. On her way up mountains, Fanny also made maps, took photographs, and studied the rocks and the weather. She often climbed more than 20,000 feet above sea level. Just before her fiftieth birthday, she hiked seventy-four miles across an icy glacier. A famous song tells us to "Climb Every Mountain." Fanny nearly did!

Build a mountain or glacier out of clay or papier-mâché.

From *Birthday a Day*, published by GoodYearBooks. Copyright © 1996 Stephen Currie.

Joan Baez
1941, New York

Some people said it was like satin. Others said it was more like gold. Everyone agreed that it was rich and strong. What was "it"? Joan's voice.

Joan hated piano lessons as a girl, but she did like to play the guitar. She became famous playing and singing old songs, as well as songs that she wrote herself. Though she gave concerts all over the world, Joan didn't much like stages. She preferred small theaters where she could be close to her audience. In fact, Joan was so informal that she often sang without shoes on!

Design a theater poster for a Joan Baez concert.

John Held, Jr.
1889, Utah

All through the 1920s, John drew pictures for magazines. The people he drew looked pretty silly: they had long pegs instead of noses, and they often stood in impossible positions. Besides being funny, John's drawings tell us about his time. His characters drove sports cars, watched football, and danced. The women wore huge bracelets and high heels, while men had floppy hats and fur coats. Stylish women during the Twenties were called "flappers," and no one drew flappers better than John.

Draw cartoon pictures of stylish people today.

From *Birthday a Day*, published by GoodYearBooks. Copyright © 1996 Stephen Currie.

Alexander Hamilton
1755, St. Kitts and Nevis

When Alexander was young, each American colony issued its own kind of money. You couldn't spend what you earned in one colony anywhere else. When the colonies became the United States, though, Alexander tried to change that system. If each state kept its own currency, he said, the states might not trust each other, and buying and selling goods would be so complicated no one would want to do it. He argued and argued—and won. Now there's only one kind of money used in the U.S. Thanks to Alexander, you can spend your allowance in any state you want.

Design your own paper money. Whose picture will it have?

January 12

Ira Hamilton Hayes
1923, *Arizona*

During World War II, the United States Marines captured an island called Iwo Jima. It was a terrible job. Enemy soldiers were hidden in tunnels all over the island. Guns, bombs, and explosives were everywhere. Many soldiers died.

Something good came out of that battle, though—a photograph of Ira and five other Marines raising the U.S. flag. That picture made Ira a hero. The photo was printed on a stamp and made into a statue. Though Ira became famous, he didn't think he deserved his fame. He always said he was no braver than anyone else who fought on Iwo Jima.

Draw your own stamp. What will it honor?

From *Birthday a Day*, published by GoodYearBooks. Copyright © 1996 Stephen Currie.

Ernestine Rose

1810, Poland

When Ernestine was a teenager, her mother died and left all of her money to Ernestine. Her father wasn't pleased. He told her to marry a friend of his, and give her new husband all the money instead. Ernestine hit the roof. She took her father to court, and she won the case.

It wasn't the first time Ernestine had fought unfairness. And it wasn't the last, either. Ernestine went on to live in six different countries. She worked for peace and women's rights in all of them. Ernestine had other talents too. Once she invented a way to get rid of household smells!

Write down what you would say to your father, if you were Ernestine.

January
14

Albert Schweitzer
1875, Germany

At age nine, Albert was playing the organ in church services. By age thirty, he had written several books. He was a teacher and an expert on religion. But Albert wanted to do more to help others. He promised to give the next thirty years of his life to the world. After reading about terrible diseases in Gabon, West Africa, he spent seven years studying to be a doctor. Then he went to Gabon and built a hospital, where he helped cure many sick people. And whenever Albert needed to raise more money, he went back to Europe and gave organ concerts!

Build a model of a hospital.

From *Birthday a Day*, published by GoodYearBooks. Copyright © 1996 Stephen Currie.

15

Martin Luther King, Jr.
1929, Georgia

There may not be any kings in the U.S., but Martin was a King of a different kind. Thousands of Americans loved and trusted him. When people were hurt by poverty, prejudice, or even their own fears, Martin tried to help. Even as a little boy, Martin knew that the world was not always a fair place. In a shoe store one day, Martin and his father were told to move out of a section reserved for white people only. As an adult, Martin became a preacher. He gave speeches and led marches to help improve the lives of African Americans in the South—and all of us everywhere.

Interview people who were alive when Martin was. Find out what they remember about him.

January 16

Charles Sigsbee
1845, New York

Charles was in the navy, but he loved science. He once spent two years studying the bottom of the Gulf of Mexico. Because he didn't have a submarine, he had to explore it from the surface. To measure how deep and cold the water was, Charles built complicated cups, wires, and traps. The lowest part of the Gulf is called "The Sigsbee Deep" in his honor. Charles did get involved with a war once—by accident. He commanded the *Maine,* a battleship that blew up in 1898. The U.S. blamed Spain, and war broke out. The American rallying cry was "Remember the *Maine!*"

Build a tool from cardboard that measures depth—even things deeper than a meter.

From *Birthday a Day*, published by GoodYearBooks. Copyright © 1996 Stephen Currie.

Benjamin Franklin

1706, Massachusetts

We call people with many talents "Renaissance men." Another good name might be "Franklin people." Ben was a curious child who became a curious adult. When would the next eclipse be? Ben figured it out. Interested in machinery? Ben invented musical instruments, bifocals to help people see better, and hand paddles for swimming. How about ideas? Ben founded libraries and colleges. He thought up phrases like "snug as a bug in a rug." He even helped start the U.S. Mail. And, oh yes, there was that little experiment with a kite. . . .

What was the most important thing Ben did? Explain why you think so.

January 18

Daniel Hale Williams
1856, Pennsylvania

The man had been stabbed in the heart. No one gave him a chance of surviving. No doctor had ever fixed that kind of damage. But when they brought the victim to the hospital, Daniel decided to try. Without antibiotics, X rays, or high-tech instruments, Daniel sewed up the hole. Amazingly, the victim lived. Daniel had done the impossible. Almost overnight, Daniel became famous. In appreciation, the president made him chief surgeon of a Washington hospital. When Daniel retired, he had helped establish more than forty hospitals across the country.

What tools do you think Daniel had to work with? Draw them.

From *Birthday a Day*, published by GoodYearBooks. Copyright © 1996 Stephen Currie.

Edgar Allan Poe
1809, Massachusetts

At midnight every January 19th, a mysterious figure in a black cape visits Edgar's grave. Before vanishing into the darkness, the stranger leaves two things behind: a rose and a bottle of cognac, Edgar's favorite drink.

As the author of some of the earliest mystery stories, Edgar would have been pleased. His stories were full of odd and unusual events. He wrote about a whirlpool so powerful it could pull down ships, a heart that beat after its owner was dead, and a huge black raven croaking "Nevermore." If you read Edgar's stories, do it during the day, with someone else in the room!

Write your own scary story or poem. Tape it using a spooky voice.

Bessie Coleman
1896, Texas

Bessie liked to live dangerously. She was a stunt pilot. At carnivals and fairs, Bessie would do loop-the-loops in a tiny plane while people on the ground watched nervously. She'd make the plane drop suddenly and scream toward the ground—only to pull out of the dive at the last second. Stunt flying was fun, but it wasn't safe. In 1926, Bessie was killed when her controls jammed. But her memory lived on. Fifty years after her death, a club was formed for African American women interested in flying: the Bessie Coleman Aviators Association.

Make up your own amazing airplane stunt. Describe it and draw it.

January 21

Leadbelly
1888, *Louisiana*

If you see red, you're angry. If you're green with envy, you're jealous. If you've got the blues, you're sad. So what are songs about hard times— reds, greens, or blues?

Huddie Ledbetter, called "Leadbelly," knew the blues in his own life. As a boy, he worked long hours picking cotton. Later, he spent time in prison. But Leadbelly didn't just live the blues. He sang them, too, accompanying himself on the guitar. His songs had names like "Goodnight, Irene" and "I'm All Out and Down." Leadbelly also had pride. He called himself "the king of all the twelve-string guitar players of the world."

Make up your own blues song. Tape yourself singing it.

From *Birthday a Day*, published by GoodYearBooks. Copyright © 1996 Stephen Currie.

January 22

Wrong-Way Corrigan
1907, Texas

Was it a mistake, or did he do it on purpose? Douglas Corrigan flew a rusty old plane from California to New York. A few days later, he took off for home. But he didn't make it. The plane's compass was broken. Instead of going west, he flew east. No one could stop him, because the plane had no radio either. The next morning, Douglas landed. In Ireland!

"I just went the wrong way," he explained. Soon everyone had heard of the adventure of "Wrong-Way." One newspaper even printed "Hail Wrong-Way Corrigan" in mirror writing to welcome him back to the U.S.

Try writing a message in mirror writing.

From *Birthday a Day*, published by GoodYearBooks. Copyright © 1996 Stephen Currie.

John Hancock

1737, Massachusetts

J ohn is best remembered for his autograph. During colonial times, he was a merchant and a politician. When the English government put new taxes on Americans, John became an enemy of the English king, George III. For several years, John led Americans who opposed the king. In 1776, he was the first of many to sign the Declaration of Independence. Writing his name in bold, large letters, John said: "There! I guess King George will be able to read that." George could, all right. Even now, we often call a signature a "John Hancock."

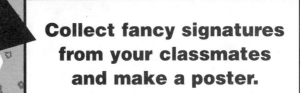

Collect fancy signatures from your classmates and make a poster.

Maria Tallchief

1925, Oklahoma

Maria was going to put her fingers to work—until her feet got in the way.

As a girl, Maria trained to be a pianist. Then she fell in love with ballet too. Once she played piano during the first half of a recital—and danced during the second. At age sixteen, she gave up music. Soon Maria was among the world's best ballerinas. Her work was called "glittery," "brilliant," and "incredible." When she retired, she made up new dances and ran her own ballet company. Not bad for a girl who might only have used her feet to push piano pedals!

Make up your own dance. Practice it in front of a mirror.

From *Birthday a Day*, published by GoodYearBooks. Copyright © 1996 Stephen Currie.

Corazón Aquino

1933, The Philippines

Things weren't going well in the Philippines. The president refused to allow elections. While many Filipinos went hungry, the president's wife owned several thousand pairs of shoes. And when Corazón's husband tried to change things, he was shot and killed.

Shocked and angry, Corazón continued his work. She formed a group called "People Power." When People Power forced the president to call an election, more than a million Filipinos signed petitions urging Corazón to run. "What do I know about being president?" Corazón asked, but she ran. She won, too—and helped bring democracy back to her country.

The official color of "People Power" was yellow. What color would you pick? Why?

January

26

Maria Von Trapp
1905, Austria

You've probably heard of Maria. She loved to sing, she lived in the Alps, she was planning to be a nun, she took care of seven children, she married their father, and the movie of her life was called *The Sound of Music*.

Maria was a real person, and most of what *The Sound of Music* says about her is true. She escaped from Austria when the Nazis came to power (though not during a concert!). Maria's family settled in Vermont, where the mountains reminded them of the Alps. Calling themselves the Trapp Family Singers, they performed Austrian folk songs all over the world.

If you could have any movie star play you, who would you choose?

From *Birthday a Day*, published by GoodYearBooks. Copyright © 1996 Stephen Currie.

January

27

Wolfgang Amadeus Mozart

1756, Austria

Wolfgang was a musical genius. By the age of four, he was an excellent pianist and a skilled composer. Throughout his childhood, he performed all over Europe. That sounds impressive enough. But people also came to see Wolfgang do musical tricks. Wolfgang could play a piece perfectly after hearing it just once. He could compose beautiful songs in only a few minutes. Audiences were always impressed. Of course, Wolfgang's father helped too. To make his son's talents seem even more amazing, he often told people that Wolfgang was two years younger than he really was!

If Wolfgang lived today, he'd get plenty of fan mail. Write him a fan letter.

January

28

Jackson Pollock
1912, Wyoming

Have you ever watched a small child paint?

If you have, Jackson's methods would look familiar. He put his canvas on the floor, not on an easel. Then he got a stick and a can of ordinary house paint. Dipping the stick into the paint, he'd drip paint all over the canvas. Sometimes he'd shake his hand back and forth, letting the paint splatter. Some people loved Jackson's work. Others had a hard time calling it "art." Jackson liked his method because he could "literally be in the painting"— which he certainly was!

Dip a marble in paint. Use a spoon to roll it on a piece of paper. What results do you get?

January 29

Oprah Winfrey
1954, Mississippi

What makes a person a good interviewer?

You have to be a good talker, of course. You need to think of good questions too. But it's even more important to be a good listener. People talk more if they think their interviewer cares about what they say. No one listened better than Oprah. Her first TV job was reading the news. But her real talent was getting people to talk about themselves and their ideas. Soon her own talk show was broadcast on stations all over the country. Next, she started her own TV production company and called it "Harpo." Why Harpo? It's Oprah—spelled backwards.

Interview someone. Write down what you learn.

January

30

Sam Loyd
1841, Pennsylvania

Sam's maze seemed simple enough. The paths were filled with letters. As you went from Start to Finish, the letters you passed spelled a sentence. Sam guaranteed that there was a solution. Yet everyone who wrote back to him replied: "There is no possible way." What was going on?

Sam made his first puzzle at age nine. By the time he died, he'd constructed thousands. Some were word or number puzzles. Others were made from wood or cardboard. To solve them, you had to work hard *and* be creative. Like the maze. As you moved through it, you did spell a sentence. The sentence was "There is no possible way"!

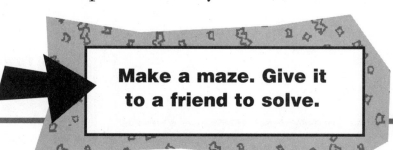

Make a maze. Give it to a friend to solve.

From *Birthday a Day*, published by GoodYearBooks. Copyright © 1996 Stephen Currie.

Jackie Robinson

1919, Georgia

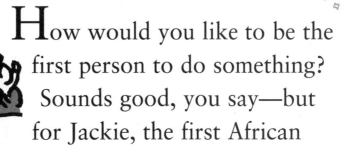

How would you like to be the first person to do something? Sounds good, you say—but for Jackie, the first African American to play major league baseball, it was very hard. Prejudiced fans booed him. Some opponents tried to hurt him. Many people thought he would never last under so much pressure.

But Jackie wouldn't let the abuse bother him. He used his bat, his speed, and his strength to show he belonged. Jackie spent ten years in the majors. By the time he retired, baseball teams were integrated for good.

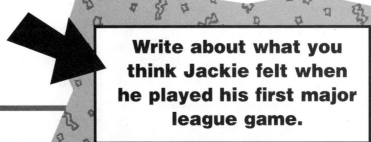

Write about what you think Jackie felt when he played his first major league game.

1

Langston Hughes
1902, Missouri

A sailor who became a poet—that was Langston. He traveled the world on ships, learning about people in different places and how they lived. Then he wrote poems about his experiences. The poems became so well known that Langston began traveling again. But this time, it was to give readings across the U.S. Many of his poems celebrate ordinary people, people who don't have much but who work hard for what they do have. In one of his most famous poems, a character says her life "ain't been no crystal stair." Neither was Langston's. But, like the people in his poems, he never gave up.

Langston wrote "Hold fast to dreams." What do you think he meant?

From *Birthday a Day*, published by GoodYearBooks. Copyright © 1996 Stephen Currie.

February

2

Jascha Heifetz
1901, Lithuania

By the time Jascha was forty-five, he had spent over a hundred thousand hours doing what he did best—playing the violin. A hundred thousand hours is close to twelve *years*. Jascha started lessons at age three. You won't be surprised to learn that he once took a whole year off to rest!

Since Jascha was such a good violinist, people all over the world wanted to hear him play. The miles he traveled could have taken him to the moon and back. Twice. All that travel was worth it, though. Jascha was so popular, he needed police guards to protect him from his enthusiastic fans!

Build your own string instrument out of cardboard and rubber bands.

From *Birthday a Day* published by GoodYearBooks. Copyright © 1996 Stephen Currie.

February 3

Elizabeth Blackwell
1821, England

In 1847 there were no women doctors in the United States. Most medical schools liked it that way. When Elizabeth applied for admission, they all turned her down. Except for one. Elizabeth packed her bags. When she arrived, however, everyone was shocked. The school had thought her application was only a joke. They had accepted her only for fun. But Elizabeth didn't leave. She made friends with other students. Two years later, she became the first woman doctor in the United States—all because no one had taken her seriously!

Draw a comic strip about Elizabeth's life.

From *Birthday a Day*, published by GoodYearBooks. Copyright © 1996 Stephen Currie.

Rosa Parks

1913, Alabama

Most people "stand up" for their rights. Rosa sat down for hers.

One day, Rosa refused to give up her seat on a bus when the driver told her to. The seat was reserved for white people only. Rosa was arrested. The African Americans in her town rallied around Rosa, who had fought racism for years. They stopped riding buses until changes were made. Many of Rosa's neighbors had to walk miles or ask for rides. As for Rosa, she lost her job. So did her husband. Her family got threatening phone calls too. But she didn't give in. For not standing up, she became "the mother of the freedom movement."

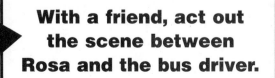

With a friend, act out the scene between Rosa and the bus driver.

February 5

Belle Starr
1848, Missouri

Belle was the leader of a band of horse thieves.

There are dozens of stories about Belle. Some say Belle played the piano beautifully. Others say her house was too small for a piano, and she didn't know how to play one anyway. Some say she dressed in fancy clothes, robbed travelers politely, and gave money to the poor. Others say she was mean and violent, and even beat up her own children. Who's right? Let's just say that she was more like Cinderella's stepmother than Robin Hood! When she died, a bell and star were carved onto her tombstone.

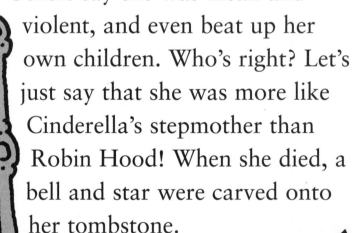

Draw what you think Belle looked like. Don't forget Venus, her horse!

From *Birthday a Day*, published by GoodYearBooks. Copyright © 1996 Stephen Currie.

Mary Leakey

1913, England

Mary got to work on the world's most exciting jigsaw puzzle.

An expert on prehistoric humans, Mary was in Africa when she discovered some bone fragments she'd never seen before. She knew right away that they were extremely old. In her excitement, she ran back to her tent screaming, "I've got him! I've got him!" The four hundred pieces fit together to make most of the skull of a human ancestor called Zinjanthropus. As if that weren't enough, Mary also studied cave paintings and discovered human footprints three million years old!

Draw a skeleton of an animal. Cut it up and have a friend put it together.

Laura Ingalls Wilder
1867, Wisconsin

Want to learn how to make jam, or what to feed chickens, or the best way of sewing sheets? Then read Laura's Little House books.

Laura was a pioneer girl who grew up on farms across the Midwest. When she was in her sixties, she began writing down her memories of the frontier. Laura especially liked to write about everyday life. Though her books are stories, many of the events really happened to Laura and her family: blizzards, troubles at school, living in a grass house. Her books are tremendously detailed. With the right tools, you could build a log cabin from her descriptions!

Write down a true story from when you were very young.

From *Birthday a Day*, published by GoodYearBooks. Copyright © 1996 Stephen Currie.

February

8

Jules Verne
1828, France

A boat that can circle the world—underwater. An invention that can travel to the moon. A flying machine.

These ideas probably don't seem very exciting to you. After all, submarines, rockets, and airplanes have already been invented. But in Jules's time, they hadn't yet been invented. Jules was a writer who was fascinated by science. He imagined how machines like these could be used, and he wrote books about them. Many of the inventions he wrote about were built not long afterwards. Not all, though— no one's figured out a way to take a *Journey to the Center of the Earth!*

Design a vehicle that could take you to the Earth's center.

Lydia Pinkham

1819, Massachusetts

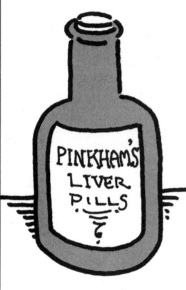

Do you have headaches, stomach problems, or a sore back? Perhaps Lydia's Vegetable Compound medicine can cure you. But don't bet on it.

Lydia's husband was owed twenty-five dollars by a man who couldn't pay. Instead, he gave the Pinkhams a recipe for a medicine made from roots, herbs, and plenty of alcohol. It seemed to make Lydia healthier, so she opened a factory and made medicines based on that recipe: Pinkham's Liver Pills, Pinkham's Blood Purifier, and many more. They rarely worked. But enough Americans believed in Lydia's medicines to make her as rich as she was healthy.

Make up a recipe for your own medicine. Don't try it!

From *Birthday a Day*, published by GoodYearBooks. Copyright © 1996 Stephen Currie.

10

William Allen White
1868, Kansas

As a teenager, William needed a job. He applied to a grocery, a dry cleaner, and a newspaper. Only the newspaper wrote back, so William became a reporter. It was a wise choice. William was an excellent writer. He kept things simple and clear. Soon he was running his own paper, the *Emporia Gazette*. The *Gazette* was small but influential. It was so influential, in fact, that he was soon offered a job in a bigger city. But William said that leaving the *Gazette* would feel like murdering his grandmother with her own crutches. And so he stayed.

What's new in school? Make the front page of a newspaper.

February 11

Thomas Alva Edison
1847, Ohio

What makes someone a genius?

According to Thomas, it was very simple: hard work. Genius, he used to say, "is 1% inspiration and 99% perspiration." As a boy, Thomas constantly asked questions. If adults answered "I don't know," Thomas would shoot back, "Why don't you know?" As an inventor, Thomas filled hundreds of notebooks with ideas. When he was inventing an electric light bulb, he tried 3,000 wrong ways before finding one that worked. In all, Thomas obtained 1,093 patents for inventions. Not a single one, he said, came by accident or by luck.

What do you think was the most important invention ever? Why?

From *Birthday a Day*, published by GoodYearBooks. Copyright © 1996 Stephen Currie.

Abraham Lincoln

1809, Kentucky

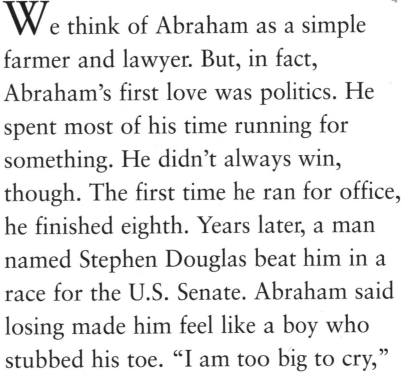

We think of Abraham as a simple farmer and lawyer. But, in fact, Abraham's first love was politics. He spent most of his time running for something. He didn't always win, though. The first time he ran for office, he finished eighth. Years later, a man named Stephen Douglas beat him in a race for the U.S. Senate. Abraham said losing made him feel like a boy who stubbed his toe. "I am too big to cry," he said, "and too badly hurt to laugh." But Abraham got the last laugh, after all. Two years later, he and Stephen ran again—for President. You know who won that time!

Make an election poster for yourself. Give people good reasons to vote for you.

February 13

Betty James
1918, Pennsylvania

Betty's husband was trying out new kinds of springs. One model he had made was sitting on a shelf when it fell off. The spring didn't just drop, though. It twisted slowly, end over end, down a pile of books. The Jameses knew right away that the product would make an excellent toy. But what should they call it? For several nights Betty went through the dictionary to find a good name. At last she reached S—and named the new toy a Slinky®. It's fun to think that if she'd been less patient, these might be called Bouncies, Crawlies, or Curlies instead.

Design your own toy. Build or draw it, and give it a good name!

From *Birthday a Day*, published by GoodYearBooks. Copyright © 1996 Stephen Currie.

George Ferris
1859, Illinois

Y ou've probably seen pictures of old riverboats with paddle-wheels that go round and round. Without those boats, the Ferris wheel might never have been built.

France had just built the Eiffel Tower, and Americans wanted something huge for their own World's Fair of 1893. George remembered the riverboats he'd seen as a boy. He built a paddlewheel you could ride, a wheel 270 feet tall that weighed 400 million pounds. Thousands of people rode it and had a great time. George's wheel wasn't as permanent as the Eiffel Tower. But then, you don't see small Eiffel Towers at carnivals all over France!

Plan a new carnival ride. Draw a diagram.

February
15

Susan B. Anthony
1820, Massachusetts

Susan always said she would rather make history than write it. In the end, she did both.

Susan worked for women's rights. At first she was ignored. Then she was considered a pest. Finally, Susan was insulted for what she believed. A newspaper even called her "repulsive." The madder people got, though, the more progress Susan knew she was making. She believed in job training for women and fair pay for the work they did. She wrote a history book about women like herself who wanted to vote. "Failure is impossible," Susan used to say. And with her determination, she might have been right.

Explain what Susan meant by "failure is impossible." Do you agree?

From *Birthday a Day*, published by GoodYearBooks. Copyright © 1996 Stephen Currie.

Edgar Bergen

1903, Illinois

As a boy, Edgar learned how to be a ventriloquist—to make his voice appear to come from somewhere else. His mother often answered the door only to find no one there. The voices on the other side were only Edgar, practicing!

As an adult, Edgar performed a show with a puppet called Charlie McCarthy. Charlie and Edgar had conversations and told jokes. Even from up close, it was hard to tell that Charlie didn't actually speak. Some said Edgar was the second most popular entertainer of his time. Who was first? Charlie. More than half of Edgar's mail came addressed to his puppet!

Make your own puppet. Get it to talk, if you can!

Marian Anderson

1902, Pennsylvania

Marian was an outstanding singer. A famous conductor had told her, "A voice like yours is heard only once in a hundred years." But when she tried to rent a hall to give a concert in Washington, D.C., the building's owners refused. Why? Because Marian was African American.

When Marian heard the news, she said, "You lose a lot of time hating people." Her friends were angry. They had Marian sing outdoors at the Lincoln Memorial instead. Seventy-five thousand people came—many more than could have fit into the other building.

Listen to a piece of music. Is it worth hearing? Write a review.

From *Birthday a Day*, published by GoodYearBooks. Copyright © 1996 Stephen Currie.

Lone Wolf
1882, Montana

Lone Wolf was a Blackfoot Indian. When he was a young man, he worked as a cowboy for a few years. But Lone Wolf preferred to draw, so he went to art school and became an artist. Using oil paints and watercolors, Lone Wolf painted the scenes he remembered from his childhood. He also made tiny sculptures out of bronze. Years after the buffaloes, horses, scouts, and cowboys of the Old West were gone, Lone Wolf's figures and paintings brought them back for everyone to see.

Use clay to make your own miniature sculptures.

February

19

Nicolaus Copernicus
1473, Poland

With one little idea, Nicolaus stopped the sun and set the Earth in motion.

For years, everyone believed that the Earth was the center of the universe. While the Earth stayed still, the sun, stars, and planets traveled around it. The idea made sense. After all, people saw the sun rise and set every day. But no one could feel the Earth whizzing through space.

Then Nicolaus came along. His hobby was astronomy. What he saw convinced him that the Earth actually moved around the sun instead. It was just one idea, but it changed the way we thought about the whole universe.

> **Design an imaginary solar system. Name the planets.**

Angelina Grimke

1805, South Carolina

Like most of her friends, Angelina hated slavery. Unlike those friends, though, Angelina had experienced slavery firsthand. Her parents had owned slaves and treated them badly. When they refused to change their ways, Angelina and her sister moved to Pennsylvania. They gave lectures and wrote about the evils of slavery. Her speeches and pamphlets were popular in the North. But when her writings reached South Carolina, postmasters burned them. Like the Northern audiences, they could tell that Angelina knew what she was talking about!

Write about a time when you saw something that was unfair.

February

21

Barbara Jordan
1936, Texas

Barbara was the first African American Congresswoman from her state. Soon after joining Congress, she got involved in a big debate. The president had broken some laws. He said that important people, like himself, were allowed to break even the Constitution if they needed to. But Barbara said that presidents had to follow the same rules as everyone else. So many people agreed with her that the president was forced to resign. Barbara was pleased—and relieved. "My faith in the Constitution is whole," Barbara said in a famous speech.

Can the president break the Constitution? Write why or why not.

From *Birthday a Day*, published by GoodYearBooks. Copyright © 1996 Stephen Currie.

George Washington

1732, Virginia

George? You know about George. He was the first king of the United States, right?

Well, no, he wasn't, but he could have been. After the Revolutionary War, Americans disagreed about the kind of government the new country should have. Many people still felt that having a king would be best. Some wanted to bring in a prince from Germany or Austria. Others said that George should get to be the first king instead. But George refused. He was glad he did. Eight years as president was more than enough for him. And being king means ruling for life!

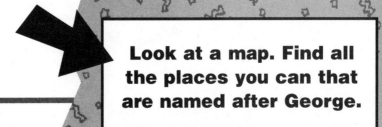

Look at a map. Find all the places you can that are named after George.

W. E. B. DuBois

1868, Massachusetts

A "crisis" means a very serious problem. W. E. B. edited a magazine called *The Crisis*. That gives you some idea how well he thought the world was working! In W. E. B.'s eyes, racism was "the problem of the 20th century." Some African American leaders argued that everyone could advance through hard work, education, and more jobs, even if discrimination continued. W. E. B. reminded them that African Americans had rights, too, just like other citizens of the United States. The crisis of racism didn't end during W. E. B.'s life, but he set up organizations that continue to fight it to this day.

What do you think will be "the problem of the 21st century"? Why?

Wilhelm Grimm

1786, Germany

Wilhelm and his brother traveled across Germany, asking poor people to tell them old stories. You've heard of them: Cinderella, Red Riding Hood, Snow White. . . . The brothers wrote down exactly what they were told. Then they published the stories as *Grimm's Fairy Tales*.

Or so they said. But the Grimms didn't tell the truth. Most of their stories actually came from rich people in France. The brothers made plenty of changes to stories they didn't like too. Still, the tales are well-known—though the Grimms' story of how they got them has been called the biggest fairy tale of them all!

> **Write a modern version of *Cinderella*. Act it out with your classmates.**

From *Birthday a Day*, published by GoodYearBooks. Copyright © 1996 Stephen Currie.

Ibn Battuta
1304, Morocco

During the 1300s, few people traveled much. The world was a dangerous and threatening place. Most people believed in giants, sea monsters, and fierce humans with the faces of dogs.

But Ibn Battuta wasn't so sure. He spent his life traveling through Africa, Asia, and Europe, writing down what he saw. Of course, he found no evidence for any of these stories. Did the books he wrote stop people from telling those tales? No. It was too much fun to talk about countries where people's ears hung down to their knees—even if Ibn Battuta said it wasn't true.

Make up an amazing story about people in imaginary countries.

From *Birthday a Day*, published by GoodYearBooks. Copyright © 1996 Stephen Currie.

Levi Strauss

1829, Germany

Levi was a traveling salesperson. When he arrived in California at the time of the Gold Rush, he brought along plenty of blue canvas cloth. He hoped to make it into tents and sell them to miners. But one miner had a better idea. "Turn that good cloth into strong pants," he advised Levi. The idea made sense. The men who panned for gold had to crouch in chilly mountain streams. The cold and moisture soon began to tear their pants apart. So Levi sewed a few sturdy pairs. They were such a hit, Levi went into the pants business full-time. Levi's jeans had been born.

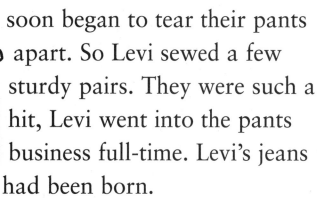

Choose three things you like to do. Design good clothes for each.

February 27

Alice Hamilton
1869, New York

Alice was a doctor, and she was worried. It seemed that her patients were being poisoned. Something in the air was slowly killing them—but what?

A visit to the factory where her patients worked helped Alice answer that question. Fumes from dangerous chemicals were everywhere. Factory owners knew the fumes might be dangerous. But they didn't clean things up. The government wasn't any help, either. Even doctors weren't doing much about the problem. Alice decided to change things— and she did. Her studies of factory conditions led to new laws which helped keep workers healthy.

Research information and write about an air pollution problem of today.

From *Birthday a Day*, published by GoodYearBooks. Copyright © 1996 Stephen Currie.

Mary Lyon

1797, Massachusetts

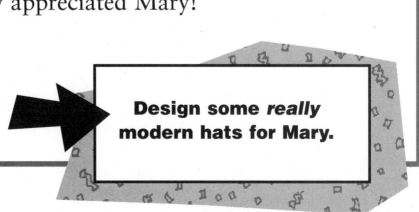

Mary wasn't much for style. For her forty-first birthday, her students gave her some fancy new hats. Her old ones were hopelessly out-of-date. But then, Mary had other things to worry about. In a time when girls usually didn't have more than a high school education, she set up a college just for women. Though many men (and women) scoffed, Mary raised money, planned lessons, and got students to enroll. She hired the best professors she could find too. Mary's students may not have appreciated her hats, but they certainly appreciated Mary!

Design some *really* modern hats for Mary.

From *Birthday a Day*, published by GoodYearBooks. Copyright © 1996 Stephen Currie.

Gioacchino Rossini
1792, Italy

"Where does the Lone Ranger take his garbage?"

"To the dump, to the dump, to the dump, dump, dump. . . ."

Actually, the "Lone Ranger" music has nothing to do with cowboys. Gioacchino composed it for his opera "William Tell"—which is set in Switzerland! Gioacchino wrote plenty of music. He worked best when he had a deadline. Once he wrote an opera in just two weeks. He finished another opera the day it was performed. The theater manager locked him up until it was done! Gioacchino made so much money from music, he quit composing at age thirty-seven and became a gourmet cook instead.

Listen to a piece of music. Write or draw what it makes you think of.

Harry Belafonte

1927, New York

Harry was a maintenance man in an apartment building. One day a tenant gave him a ticket to a play. It was the first play Harry had ever seen, and it changed his life. Soon afterward, he quit his job to become an actor. He also studied and performed old folk songs. His specialties were bouncy "calypso" songs from Jamaica, where he spent part of his childhood. Calypso music uses tricky rhythms and homemade instruments. Harry became so popular, some people thought he had invented calypso—which he hadn't. By the way, what's gray and sings? Harry Elafonte, of course!

Make your own "calypso" drum or stringed instrument. Play it.

Sarah Royce
1819, England

As a pioneer in California, Sarah had a difficult time. She and her husband never had much money. At one point the whole family had to live in a tent. But Sarah never got discouraged. If something needed to be done, she did it. Once she lived in an area without schools, so she started one herself. She taught all of the classes too. Another place had no churches. Instead of waiting for someone else to build a church, she brought traveling ministers to her house and invited the community in. Spunky women like Sarah helped create towns and villages on the American frontier.

Imagine you were a pioneer. Choose eight things to take along.

From *Birthday a Day*, published by GoodYearBooks. Copyright © 1996 Stephen Currie.

March
3

Jackie Joyner-Kersee
1962, Illinois

Jackie was named for Jackie Kennedy, who once was First Lady of the United States. Jackie's grandmother said that Jackie was bound to be the first lady of *something* too. She was right. Could you jump higher than your head? Jackie could. How about leaping twenty-five feet through the air? Jackie could do that too. A champion track star, Jackie held world records in both running and jumping events. It was quite a "leap" for a girl who finished dead last in her first track meet, back when she was only nine years old!

Estimate how far you could jump. Try it and measure. How close were you?

Garrett Morgan

1875, Kentucky

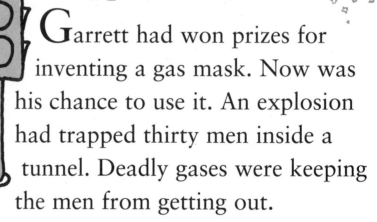

Garrett had won prizes for inventing a gas mask. Now was his chance to use it. An explosion had trapped thirty men inside a tunnel. Deadly gases were keeping the men from getting out.

Garrett slid on a mask and gave masks to other rescuers too. Even in the tunnel, the masks let them breathe pure oxygen. One by one, nearly every man was brought to safety. The gas masks had done their work. Factories ordered dozens. So did the Army. Garrett got rich and bought himself a car. When he grew disgusted with accidents and traffic, he went on to invent the stoplight!

Make up a skit explaining why Garrett invented the traffic light.

From *Birthday a Day*, published by GoodYearBooks. Copyright © 1996 Stephen Currie.

5

Mercator
1512, Belgium

You can't draw a perfect map of the world on a flat piece of paper. But Mercator figured out a way to come close. First, he imagined a clear globe with the outlines of countries drawn on the surface and a light inside. Then, he imagined a paper cylinder around that globe. The light would cast the shadows of the countries onto the paper. Ink in the shadows, unroll the paper, and you had Mercator's map. Some countries came out the wrong size, but shapes and directions were so accurate that sailors and geographers used it for years.

**Look at a globe.
Copy the continents
onto flat paper.**

Michelangelo Buonarroti

1475, Italy

Though Michelangelo painted and wrote poetry, he thought of himself as a sculptor. Once he lived for eight months in a rock quarry, trying to find the perfect block of marble for a statue. One sculpture, the "David," was carved from a single piece of marble fourteen feet high. Michelangelo's figures were perfectly proportioned. You can almost see the muscles flex and bulge. Stone arms hang from bodies just the way real arms would. How did Michelangelo know so much about the human form? As a young man, he spent lots of time examining dead bodies in a hospital!

Draw a picture of a friend. Try to get the body in perfect proportion.

From *Birthday a Day*, published by GoodYearBooks. Copyright © 1996 Stephen Currie.

Janet Guthrie

1938, Iowa

Can you be careful and daring at the same time? Janet was!

As a teenager, Janet could fly twenty different kinds of planes. She even thought about being an astronaut. Instead, she became a scientist with a special interest in flight. Then she bought a used sports car. After rebuilding its engine, Janet got hooked on auto racing. You have to take chances to win races. But when you travel almost two hundred miles an hour, you need to use common sense too. Janet did both. She won many times. In 1977 she was the first woman to compete in the Indianapolis 500.

Design your own race car. Draw it.

March

8

Kenneth Grahame
1859, Scotland

Mr. Toad, in Kenneth's book *The Wind in the Willows,* is one of the most loudmouthed, irresponsible heroes of any children's story. He drives his car recklessly. He's rude to his friends. He even insults the police and tries to escape from jail. Kenneth was not like Mr. Toad at all. He worked in a bank. Dressed in a fine suit and tie, he spent his time counting money and talking about loans. Even after Toad made Kenneth famous, Kenneth kept his bank job. It's fun to imagine Toad having to deal politely with people all day long— just as his creator did.

Write a story about a character who is your complete opposite.

From *Birthday a Day*, published by GoodYearBooks. Copyright © 1996 Stephen Currie.

9

Bobby Fischer
1943, Illinois

Bobby became famous by moving wood better than anyone else.

No, he wasn't a lumberjack or a sculptor. He played chess. His sister taught him the rules when he was six. By age fourteen, he was the U.S. champion. Before long, he was the best in the world. But Bobby could be difficult. He often accused his opponents of cheating. If he didn't like the referee, the lights, or his chair, he'd walk out. At last he refused to play matches at all because he felt everyone was out to get him. Was Bobby's style of play like other people's? Nope. It was as unusual as he was!

Teach someone how to play chess. If you don't know the rules, ask someone to teach you.

From *Birthday a Day*, published by GoodYearBooks. Copyright © 1996 Stephen Currie.

Pauline Johnson
1861, Ontario

Pauline called her most famous book *The Song My Paddle Sings*—but she wasn't a rower or a Ping-Pong player. The title referred to the Mohawk Indians, who had paddled canoes for centuries. Pauline was a poet with a special interest in her Mohawk ancestry. "By right, by birth," she wrote in one poem, "we Indians own these lands."

As a girl, Pauline was too shy to show anyone her work. But that soon changed. Pauline's poetry made her famous. Once she traveled to a few towns to read her poems. She was so popular that she stayed on tour for fifteen years!

Imagine paddling a canoe. Write words that describe how it might feel.

From *Birthday a Day*, published by GoodYearBooks. Copyright © 1996 Stephen Currie.

March
11

Bobby McFerrin
1950, New York

So the horn players in your band never showed up, and the guy who plays the sax is on vacation. What to do? Don't worry—call Bobby!

Bobby was trained as a pianist, but his voice made him famous. He could do amazing things with it. Can you produce the sound of radio static? Bobby could. He could also play all the parts in *The Wizard of Oz,* sing the sound of a violin, or imitate an entire jazz band. When he started doing a one-man show, his friends thought he'd never succeed. But Bobby proved them wrong. His act was funny, dramatic, and musical, and audiences loved it.

Imitate the sounds of some instruments with your voice. Make a recording of the sounds.

March
12

Virginia Hamilton
1936, Ohio

Where do writers get their ideas?

Many of Virginia's books came from her own experience. One book told about growing up around plenty of cousins—just as Virginia had done. Another dealt with an interracial family; Virginia was African American, and her husband was white. Others came from family history. Virginia's grandfather had been a runaway slave. He told his children stories about slavery "so that it will never happen to you," and Virginia used some of the stories in her own books. "My stories," she said once, "are little pieces of me."

➤ **Write a story based on some "little pieces" of your experiences.**

From *Birthday a Day*, published by GoodYearBooks. Copyright © 1996 Stephen Currie.

Salote Tupou
1900, Tonga

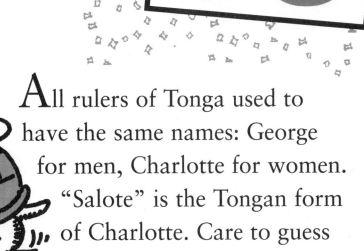

All rulers of Tonga used to have the same names: George for men, Charlotte for women. "Salote" is the Tongan form of Charlotte. Care to guess what her job was?

As queen, Salote worked to give every Tongan medical care, an education, and a free plot of land. On her fiftieth birthday, Salote threw a huge party, inviting all fifty thousand Tongans. Most of them came. They brought pigs, vegetables, and fish to help her celebrate. Another Tongan was there as well: the palace tortoise. According to legend, the tortoise had been a present too—to a Tongan king two hundred years before!

Plan your own birthday feast. What will you serve? What decorations will you use?

March

14

Albert Einstein
1879, Germany

Imagine you're in a bright room with no windows and the door closed. Now imagine that you turn the light switch off. The room becomes dark. Where did the light go?

Questions like these used to bother Albert. When he grew up he explored similar ideas. Could anything travel faster than light? What was at the edge of the universe? How was space related to time? Albert's answers led to some important—and unexpected— scientific theories. Albert liked art, and he played the violin, but "what's really beautiful," he used to say, "is science!"

Explain what you think happens to the light in a room when it's turned off.

From *Birthday a Day*, published by GoodYearBooks. Copyright © 1996 Stephen Currie.

Andrew Jackson
1767, *South Carolina*

When Andrew became president, he threw a party to celebrate. Most of the guests were ordinary people, and they had a blast. They climbed in the windows, tracked mud through the White House, and smashed up some china. Andrew didn't especially mind. He was a rough frontiersman himself. Born poor, he had become rich without getting much education or manners. All the presidents before Andrew were wealthy gentlemen who had gone to college. Andrew broke the pattern! Some thought he disgraced the presidency, but others loved him, and he served two terms.

Draw before-and-after pictures of the White House.

Jean Rosenthal
1912, New York

After Jean signed up for theater school, she realized that she didn't want to be an actress. But she found something else to love about the theater—lights.

In those days, theater lights were only used to brighten the stage and show off scenery. Jean had other ideas. She used lights to set the mood for a show. Spooky scenes might need dark colors, while bouncy songs would have bright, cheerful lighting. Jean set up lights on the side of the stage, too, to make actors look more three-dimensional. Her work was so good, she was once asked to design lights to make an airport terminal seem cozy!

> **Make a chart of the colors you see when you shine a flashlight through colored tissue paper.**

From *Birthday a Day*, published by GoodYearBooks. Copyright © 1996 Stephen Currie.

March

17

Kate Greenaway
1846, England

Kate was twelve when she decided to become an artist. She started with valentines and Christmas cards. Next, she wrote and illustrated children's books. Kate took great pride in the clothes that appeared in her drawings. Her characters were always well dressed. Some of the styles she drew even started fashion trends; one company actually manufactured a "Kate Greenaway Shoe." Most artists just imagine what they want their characters to be wearing. Not Kate. She rarely started to draw a picture until she had sewed the proper clothes herself and dressed a model in them!

Choose a familiar story. Illustrate it.

Anna Held

1865, Poland

There's a lot we don't know about Anna— because Anna wanted it that way. Anna was a singer and actress. She felt that being mysterious would make people notice her. So Anna made up stories about her life and spread them around. Was Anna Catholic or Jewish? Did she really take a milk bath every day? What was her mother's real name? No one knew for sure, and Anna wasn't saying. Sometimes she answered the exact same question in different ways. All anyone knew was that Anna was one of the most popular stars of her time. And the mysteries surrounding her didn't hurt her popularity a bit.

Make up a story about your own life. Try to convince someone it's true.

March

19

William Jennings Bryan

1860, Illinois

William was a terrific speaker. People came from miles away to hear him talk. His voice was strong, and he knew how to get his audience excited. One of William's speeches actually got him nominated for president. Not everyone agreed with his views, though. William ran three times, and he lost all three. Still, William and his family kept their sense of humor. Once his daughter had to dash to catch a train before it pulled out. "Well, anyhow," she said to a friend as she settled into her seat, "*one* of the Bryans has run for something and caught it."

➤ **Make up another joke about William losing so often.**

Mitsumasa Anno

1926, Japan

What letters stay the same when you turn them upside down? How about when you put them up against a mirror?

Mitsumasa enjoyed problems like these. His books, from *Topsy-Turvies* to *Anno's Mysterious Multiplying Jar,* showed how math and art connect. Some books asked readers to find certain numbers of objects in a picture. It's harder than it looks! Others used art to explore patterns, combinations, or enormous numbers. Any guesses about Mitsumasa's favorite subjects in school? That's right. Math and art.

Solve the problems at the top of the page. Print the letters on paper.

From *Birthday a Day* published by GoodYearBooks. Copyright © 1996 Stephen Currie.

March

21

J. S. Bach
1685, Germany

As a young man, J. S. was offered a great job playing the organ. But he turned it down. There was a catch. The new organist had to marry the old organist's daughter.

While J. S. was alive, he was better known as an organist than as a composer. In fact, many of his compositions were lost during his lifetime. But there's a lot left over. For several years J. S. wrote a complete cantata every week—a vocal piece about half an hour long—and still had time left over for sonatas, concertos, fugues, trios, partitas, preludes, arias, masses, suites, pastorales, oratorios, quartets. . . .

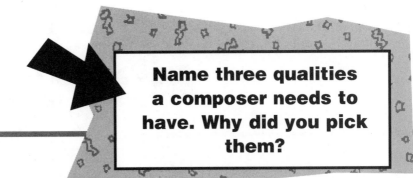

Name three qualities a composer needs to have. Why did you pick them?

Marcel Marceau
1923, France

Would you like to hear an audio tape of Marcel performing?

Don't bother—it would be very dull. Marcel was a mime—an actor who stays silent through his performance. Even without sounds or special props, Marcel could make it appear that he was walking into a strong wind, climbing stairs, or catching butterflies. Pick up a chair and notice how your body moves. Now "mime" the movements without using a real chair. Did your body do the same thing? Suppose the chair were heavier? After years of practice like this, Marcel was the best-known mime in the world.

Mime an activity for a friend. Can your friend guess what you're doing?

From *Birthday a Day*, published by GoodYearBooks. Copyright © 1996 Stephen Currie.

March
23

Fannie Farmer
1857, Massachusetts

When Fannie was young, she was the worst cook in her family. She would start a pot boiling and forget all about it. But it was Fannie who taught cooking as an adult—and who became famous for writing a cookbook.

Before Fannie's cookbook, cooks used a lot of guesswork. Recipes called for "butter the size of a hazelnut" or "a handful of flour." People whose hands (or hazelnuts) were different sizes got different foods. But Fannie used exact measurements. She traded in "pinches" and "dashes" for "teaspoons" and "cups," and made it possible for anyone to cook according to a recipe.

With an adult, follow a recipe twice, once exact and once "close."

Harry Houdini

1874, Hungary

Lock Harry in jail—he'd escape. Tie him up, put him in a box, toss him in the water—he'd be back. Partly, Harry did it with fake locks and handcuffs. But he really could do amazing things. Harry trained himself to hold his breath far longer than most people could. That certainly helped his underwater escapes! He could unlock a door with a piece of wire held between his toes. He untied knots with his teeth. Harry even developed his throat muscles so he could half-swallow a key and spit it out when he needed it. (Don't try this at home!) He was the greatest escape artist the world has ever known.

Plan your own escape. Draw it.

From *Birthday a Day*, published by GoodYearBooks. Copyright © 1996 Stephen Currie.

March

25

Gutzon Borglum
1867, Idaho

"Our age," Gutzon predicted, "will be called 'The COLOSSAL Age.'" A sculptor who ran away from home at age twelve, Gutzon was asked to carve a monument onto Mount Rushmore in South Dakota. His idea was COLOSSAL: the heads of four presidents, so huge that their lips would be eighteen feet long. To blast and cut the rock, workers hung from seats fastened to the top of the mountain. Gutzon's temper was COLOSSAL too. When things went wrong, he fired everyone in sight, only to hire them back the next day. He expected the project to last five years, but instead it took a COLOSSAL fourteen.

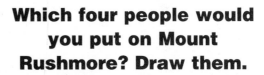

Which four people would you put on Mount Rushmore? Draw them.

Sandra Day O'Connor
1930, Texas

The highest court in the country isn't on top of a mountain. It's the Supreme Court in Washington. What this court says, goes. All nine justices on the Supreme Court wear black robes and decide cases together. Supreme Court judges are usually old and experienced. Until 1981, they were alike in another way too: all of them were men. Sandra changed that. She had been a lawyer, a lawmaker, and a judge, and President Ronald Reagan appointed her to the Supreme Court. Sandra was all set to go: her car's license plate read JUEZA—"judge" in Spanish.

Design your own license plate. What will it say?

From *Birthday a Day*, published by GoodYearBooks. Copyright © 1996 Stephen Currie.

March

27

Patty Smith Hill
1868, Kentucky

Patty's parents wanted her to study things that were interesting to her. When Patty became a teacher, she tried out the same idea on her class. Instead of using worksheets, she had children plant gardens, build with blocks, and play games they enjoyed.

Patty and her sister also wrote a song for the children, which they called "Good Morning to All." Later on, they added new words. The new version became the song that is sung most often in the United States today. Stumped? It was "Happy Birthday to You."

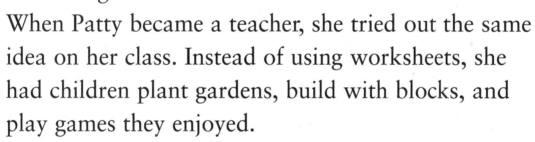

Make up new words to "Happy Birthday." Sing them on tape.

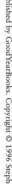

March

28

Marlin Perkins

1905, Missouri

Young Marlin was the proud owner of a dog—and rabbits, squirrels, goats, and opossums. His pets were very unpopular. The neighbors called him "that awful Perkins boy," and his teacher was not pleased when Marlin put a snake in the classroom closet. If they'd known that Marlin was just practicing to be a zookeeper, they might have been nicer. (Then again, maybe not.)

As part of his job, Marlin filmed TV programs about zoos. At first he brought animals to the studio. But they kept catching cold, so he filmed it at the zoo instead. Just as well. Imagine a sneezing giraffe!

Plan your own zoo. Which animals will it have?

March

29

Frances Jacobs
1843, Kentucky

If you smelled soap in Denver, Colorado, you could tell Frances was coming. Everywhere she went, Frances carried bars to give to anyone who needed a bath. More important, though, were the money and food she brought to people who didn't have enough. Frances was a charity worker. She spent her time in the poorest section of Denver. Mud, rain, snow, or dust, Frances waded through to help people in need. Some of her friends said that visiting the poor was disgusting, but others knew better. When Colorado chose its greatest settlers, Frances was one of the first honored.

Make a list of five things you can do to help people in need.

30

Vincent Van Gogh
1853, The Netherlands

Vincent frightened people. He'd walk around town in a dirty blue smock and a hat that didn't fit. He lost his job at an art gallery because he kept arguing with the customers. Once he cut off part of his ear and gave it to a woman he loved. She barely knew who he was.

Yet Vincent was a great painter. His bright colors seem to jump off the canvas at you. During his time, Vincent's paintings seemed very unusual. For nine years, he couldn't sell a single picture. No longer. Today, his paintings of sunflowers and the night sky would cost millions—if their owners would part with them!

Paint your own picture. Use only bright colors.

From Birthday a Day, published by GoodYearBooks. Copyright © 1996 Stephen Currie.

March

31

Cesar Chavez
1927, Arizona

Imagine that you work out in the sun all day, with hardly any time off. Your pay is low and your house is cramped and run-down. And if you complain, you might lose your job.

That was Cesar's life. He was a migrant worker, a person who traveled from farm to farm picking fruits and vegetables. As an adult, he organized migrants into a union. Together they went to farmers to demand better pay and working conditions. Cesar even got shoppers to stop buying grapes and lettuce till the farmers gave in. The strategy worked. Life is still hard for migrants, but things are better than they used to be.

Choose a fruit or vegetable. Do research to find out where it grows.

April 1

P. D. Q. Bach
1742, Germany

The great composer J. S. Bach had many children. P. D. Q. was the last—and the least. P. D. Q. tried to compose music, but he couldn't do it right. When other composers were writing music for pianos, trumpets, and violins, P. D. Q. wrote for the bicycle, the foghorn, and the kazoo. He even wrote music to be played on a piece of pasta. But don't feel too sorry for him. P. D. Q. never existed. He was the invention of a composer named Peter Schickele, who wrote and recorded P. D. Q.'s "music." Peter chose the first of April to be P. D. Q.'s birthday, which made sense: Happy April Fools' Day!

Invent an imaginary person. Write his or her life story.

From *Birthday a Day*, published by GoodYearBooks. Copyright © 1996 Stephen Currie.

2

Hans Christian Andersen

1805, Denmark

Y̶ou know Hans for his fairy tales: stories like *The Ugly Duckling* and *The Little Mermaid*. But Hans would rather be remembered as a poet and playwright. Of course, Hans had a little trouble with his plays. The first time he wrote one, he killed off all the characters. When he sent another play to be performed, the producers wrote back and said it was obvious that Hans didn't know anything. His teacher called Hans's poetry "terrible." Fortunately, Hans kept on writing and became a success. He wrote the fairy tales for fun—and was surprised to see how popular they became.

Write a short play. Don't kill off all the characters!

April

3

Jane Goodall
1934, England

For years no one knew much about chimpanzees. Wild chimps usually got nervous and ran away from scientists. When Jane went off to study them herself, other animal experts didn't expect much. But Jane had a plan. Before trying to study the chimps, she let them get used to being near her. Jane even imitated a chimp, climbing trees and eating a few insects! It took incredible patience, but after two years the chimps took no more notice of her. That was Jane's chance. She saw how chimps raised their families, how they used tools, how they ate, and much more that no scientist had ever seen before.

Watch an animal for fifteen minutes. Write down everything it does.

From *Birthday a Day*, published by GoodYearBooks. Copyright © 1996 Stephen Currie.

4

Maya Angelou
1928, Missouri

Maya liked to do things the old-fashioned way. Though she was a writer, Maya didn't use computers or even a typewriter. Instead, she wrote everything by hand, on ruled yellow paper. Her books tell about dreams and failures. They celebrate the human spirit. When Bill Clinton became president, Maya was asked to read one of her poems. People liked the poem, but they especially remembered the way Maya read it. Her strong and resonant voice grabbed the audience's attention. Someone said later that Maya could probably make even the back of a cereal box sound interesting!

Read something very boring out loud. Make it as interesting as you can.

April 5

Maria Martinez
1884, New Mexico

For centuries Pueblo Indians had been making beautiful pots out of coiled clay. Like other Pueblo girls, Maria grew up making pots. But by the time she was born, some of the ancient methods and traditions had been forgotten.

Maria was curious about the old ways. She studied ancient pots, talked to other Native Americans, and experimented. Her original pottery, based on ancient designs, soon became famous. She even figured out how to make a deep black finish that her ancestors had frequently used, and she used it to decorate her own pots too.

Make a pot out of clay. Draw designs in the sides with a toothpick.

From *Birthday a Day*, published by GoodYearBooks. Copyright © 1996 Stephen Currie.

Jim Beckwourth

1798, Virginia

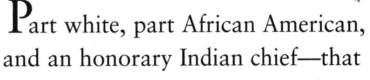

Part white, part African American, and an honorary Indian chief—that was Jim. Jim lived on the frontier. He explored, scouted, and trapped beavers. Beavers? Well, beaver fur was very popular for making hats and coats. A good trapper could make lots of money, and Jim was an expert.

Though Jim loved the frontier, it could be a dangerous place. Jim's friends told plenty of stories about Jim's adventures: how he rescued trappers from icy water, how he outwitted angry bears, how he ran miles to escape from enemies. Some of the stories may even be true!

Make up your own story of Jim's frontier adventures.

W. K. Kellogg
1860, Michigan

When W. K. was a boy, Americans ate hot breakfasts—foods such as ham, fish, and roast beef. W. K. and his brother believed that wheat, oats, and corn were healthier for breakfast. They had their own recipe. They cooked grain, ran it through rollers, and ground the rolled dough into meal. It looked kind of mushy, but it tasted all right. Then one day they cooked some grain and left it on the stove by accident. It dried up, but W. K. rolled it out anyway, just to see what would happen. To his surprise, the grain turned into tasty little flakes. W. K. had invented cornflakes—and changed American breakfasts.

Ask people their favorite brand of cereal. Make a graph to show what you found out.

April

8

Sonja Henie
1912, Norway

To fight World War II, the U.S. government needed tons of steel. That left very little for ordinary use. Sonja worried that she wouldn't be able to replace the steel blades of her ice skates if they broke. So she insured her skates—for $250,000!

It made sense. Sonja's skates weren't toys. They were her livelihood. Sonja was the first figure skater to bring dance steps into her routines. She went on to win three Olympic gold medals and ten world championships. Later on, she ran her own ice show and starred in movies—on skates, of course.

Skaters often form geometric figures as they skate. Draw some figures skaters could make.

From *Birthday a Day*, published by GoodYearBooks. Copyright © 1996 Stephen Currie.

Ellen Smith Tupper

1822, Rhode Island

Of all the bees in a hive, the queen is most important. The other bees protect her and make sure she is fed. Seem unfair? There's a reason. Only the queen produces children.

Ellen knew more about bees than almost anyone. She kept beehives all over her farm. For years she observed bees, wrote about bees, and taught about bees. She studied the way bees dance to communicate with each other. For her knowledge, Ellen was nicknamed "The Queen Bee"—even though she only produced five children, and a real queen might produce two thousand every day.

Go on an insect hunt. How many can you find?

From *Birthday a Day*, published by GoodYearBooks. Copyright © 1996 Stephen Currie.

April

10

Omar Sharif
1932, Egypt

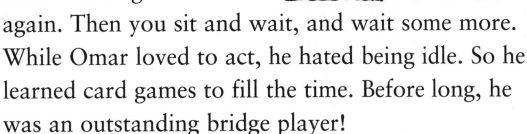

Moviemaking may seem glamorous, but it's often deadly dull. You shoot the same scene again and again. Then you sit and wait, and wait some more. While Omar loved to act, he hated being idle. So he learned card games to fill the time. Before long, he was an outstanding bridge player!

As a boy, Omar spent all his time at the movies. Though his parents and teachers wanted him to study business or math, Omar insisted on acting instead. He was soon one of Egypt's most popular actors. Though Omar sometimes wound up playing a bad guy, he preferred to play the hero.

> **Teach someone a card game. Write down a good strategy for winning it.**

April 11

Lillie Bliss
1864, Massachusetts

Lillie's mother was horrified when Lillie became interested in art. First of all, she didn't like the paintings: weird modern stuff by people with strange names like "Picasso" and "Monet." Worse, Lillie made friends with the artists, even though her mother hadn't met any of their families. But Mrs. Bliss came down hard. Though Lillie was forty years old, Mrs. Bliss made her keep all the paintings she bought in the attic. When Mrs. Bliss died, Lillie brought her paintings down and opened a gallery, which became the Museum of Modern Art in New York City.

Make up a skit about Lillie and her mother.

From *Birthday a Day*, published by GoodYearBooks. Copyright © 1996 Stephen Currie.

Beverly Cleary

1916, Oregon

Beverly had a hard time learning to read. Spelling made no sense to her, either. "What was that 'H' doing in 'John'?" she wondered. She was put in the lowest reading group at school and ignored. Meanwhile, the good readers got the best seats and plenty of praise. Yet Beverly didn't give up, and in the end her hard work paid off. She grew to love books. When she tried writing a few of her own, they were a hit. Children all over the country loved characters like Ramona Quimby, Henry Huggins, and Ralph S. Mouse. Beverly was astonished. Imagine what her teachers might have said!

Find ten more silly spellings. Write them down.

April

13

Thomas Jefferson
1743, Virginia

Thomas did a lot of good in the world. He was the main author of the Declaration of Independence. He wrote laws letting people worship as they liked, and he started a great university. Thomas purchased a body of land from France called the Louisiana Purchase, which eventually became parts or all of fifteen U.S. states. He designed buildings and invented a swivel chair. He even served as president, though he didn't enjoy it much and wanted that achievement left off his tombstone. But all this can't make up for Thomas's big mistake: bringing Brussels sprouts to America!

What would you want to be remembered for? Write down five things.

From *Birthday a Day*, published by GoodYearBooks. Copyright © 1996 Stephen Currie.

14

Loretta Lynn
1932, Kentucky

How would you like to write your own report card?

Loretta did. When she was an eighth grader in a one-room school, the teacher had her write everyone's reports. It wasn't much of an education. But Loretta became a country music star anyway. Writing songs was much more fun than writing report cards. When no paper was handy, Loretta wrote lyrics on napkins, bags, or even shoe boxes! Her most famous song, "Coal Miner's Daughter," told about her own childhood. To promote her first record, Loretta toured the U.S. in a run-down Ford. But before long, she had traded it in and was riding a custom-built bus.

Make up your own country song. Record it on tape.

15

Leonardo da Vinci
1452, Italy

Quick! Name a painting! Leonardo's *Mona Lisa* might be the most famous work of art around. For generations, people have wondered what the lady in the picture is smiling about. But if you saw the woman he used as a model, you might not recognize her. It seems Leonardo wasn't much good at faces!

Then again, faces were about all he couldn't do. Leonardo was an expert sculptor, musician, scientist, and engineer. His last name meant "from Vinci," the town where he lived; and centuries after his death, his name became famous again—this time, for being a Teenage Mutant Ninja Turtle.

Who would you be, if the town you lived in was your last name?

From *Birthday a Day*, published by GoodYearBooks. Copyright © 1996 Stephen Currie.

From *Birthday a Day*, published by GoodYearBooks. Copyright © 1996 Stephen Currie.

April

16

Kareem Abdul-Jabbar

1947, New York

Before Shaq, before Air Jordan, before Magic and Larry, there were other great basketball players. Like Kareem. When he began college, players rarely dunked the ball. Kareem was tall and agile, though, and he did it over and over. No one could defend against him, so the colleges banned dunks. No problem! Kareem came up with a new shot. With his back to the basket, he'd pivot, jump, and lob the ball in with one hand. No one could defend this "sky hook," either—but the colleges didn't change the rules again. By this time, they knew Kareem was one of the greatest.

How many dribbles can you do in a row? Try it. Record your results on a graph.

April 17

Mary Alexander
1693, New York

If you wanted to go shopping before the Revolution, Mary was your woman. It was unusual for women to run businesses during colonial times, but Mary was very good at it. Her husband had been a trader. When he died, she made his business even more prosperous by opening a store. Almost every ship that came to town brought cloth, tools, or furniture for Mary to sell. Then she married a lawyer. People who owed him money often paid him in goods instead. Any guesses where those goods wound up? That's right—in Mary's store!

Make your own store advertisements. What will you be selling?

Clarence Darrow
1857, Ohio

Clarence loved to argue. Especially when he knew he was certain to lose.

Clarence was a lawyer who mostly took on impossible cases. He defended ideas that were unpopular and people with tons of evidence against them. Clarence studied his cases carefully. He was a convincing speaker, and he knew how to get the newspapers on his side. Though Clarence often lost, he never gave up. In his first case, he defended a boy accused of stealing a harness worth fifteen dollars. It took eight years to settle the case, but Clarence hung on. He even won!

Write an argument for a cause you feel is right.

Glenn Seaborg

1912, Michigan

Which would you rather put on your french fries: sodium mixed with chlorine, or potassium, carbon, and nitrogen?

The universe is made up of "elements." Lead is an element; so are tin and mercury. Two elements, oxygen and hydrogen, mix to make water, and you breathe out oxygen and carbon. About ninety elements occur in nature. But Glenn produced many more. He put natural elements in a machine and shot tiny particles at them until they were something completely new. By the way, sodium and chlorine make salt, but potassium, carbon, and nitrogen are a poison called cyanide—so watch those fries!

Find a list of the elements. Mark the ones you've heard of.

From *Birthday a Day*, published by GoodYearBooks. Copyright © 1996 Stephen Currie.

April

20

Agnes Chase
1869, Illinois

Agnes became a scientist because her nephew needed help.

Her nephew had a book about wildflowers, but he couldn't figure out how to use it. He asked Agnes for help. Together they spent a day looking for flowers in a nearby field. Then they used the book to identify what they found. When Agnes's nephew moved on to other interests, Agnes didn't. She started collecting and drawing wild plants for fun. Before long, Agnes was an expert on plants. Students came from all over the world to study with her. Where did they stay? In Agnes's own house!

Go on a flower hunt. How many can you find? List their names.

John Muir

1838, Scotland

Everyone thought John was strange. During blizzards and thunderstorms, he stood outside to watch. But John was just a nature lover.

The more John learned about the earth, the angrier he got about the way it was treated. Where John saw rivers, forests, and meadows, others saw water to drink, wood to chop, and grass to feed sheep. So John started the Sierra Club, which worked to keep the natural world the way it was. Sometimes he was successful. Other times he wasn't. His biggest win, though, helped set up our system of national parks.

Draw John doing something "strange" to learn more about the environment.

From *Birthday a Day*, published by GoodYearBooks. Copyright © 1996 Stephen Currie.

Queen Isabella of Spain

1451, Spain

At first, Isabella was queen of Castile. Her husband was king of Aragon. They decided to combine their countries and call the whole thing Spain. Just as well; it doesn't sound right to say that the queen of "Aragastile" or "Castagon" sponsored Columbus's trip to the New World.

Isabella did a lot for art and learning, but her temper could be fierce. She made Columbus free his Native American slaves, but she kicked Moslems and Jews out of Spain and even had them killed. Though she was ruthless, everyone agreed that she had helped make Spain a world power.

If 1 is awful and 10 is great, where does Isabella rank? Why?

William Shakespeare

1564, England

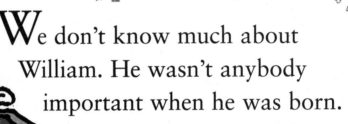

We don't know much about William. He wasn't anybody important when he was born. We aren't even positive that today is his birthday, though this is when people usually celebrate it. William grew up to be an actor and a stage manager, and—oh yes—he wrote a few plays. Have you heard of the witches in *Macbeth* and the balcony scene in *Romeo and Juliet?* William wrote them both. He also made up the lines "To be or not to be" from Hamlet and "Beware the Ides of March" from *Julius Caesar.* Most people consider William the greatest playwright in the English language.

The "witches" scene is at the beginning of *Macbeth.* Read it and act it out.

From *Birthday a Day,* published by GoodYearBooks. Copyright © 1996 Stephen Currie.

April 24

Gideon Sundback
1880, Sweden

Engineers don't just design bridges and buildings. Sometimes they work on small projects too. Gideon's great invention was a good example. First, he rounded some pieces of metal and fastened them, one by one, along two strips of cloth. He put the strips so the metal pieces faced each other, and attached another metal piece to the bottom of both sides. When he slid this piece up the strips, the round pieces from each side came together. When he slid it back, the pieces came apart. It fastened cloth better than buttons or hooks! Figured it out yet? Gideon had invented the zipper.

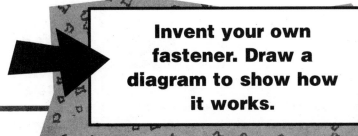

Invent your own fastener. Draw a diagram to show how it works.

From *Birthday a Day*, published by GoodYearBooks. Copyright © 1996 Stephen Currie.

Guglielmo Marconi
1874, Italy

Most people would say radios are for listening to music. But when Guglielmo invented the first radio, he didn't have Top 40 hits in mind. His radio was a "wireless telegraph"; like a walkie-talkie, it could send and receive messages. It was made especially for use at sea.

As a boy, Guglielmo built his own telegraph in the attic. After many experiments, he figured out how to send signals without wires. When he brought his radio to England, though, the customs inspectors called in the bomb squad. Guglielmo's invention had so many dials, boxes, and batteries, they thought it might explode!

Make up a skit about Guglielmo and the customs inspectors.

From *Birthday a Day*, published by GoodYearBooks. Copyright © 1996 Stephen Currie.

From *Birthday a Day*, published by GoodYearBooks. Copyright © 1996 Stephen Currie.

April

26

I. M. Pei

1917, China

When I. M. came to America to study architecture, he got a shock. His school didn't just want him to design buildings; it wanted him to paint what he thought they would look like after they were built. I. M. had never painted, so he changed to a school that didn't require painting.

Though I. M. couldn't paint, he became known for clever, artistic designs. He liked to use indoor bridges to connect different parts of buildings. A plan for a high-rise building arranged apartments in a spiral around a central elevator. Once I. M. even designed a museum in the shape of a triangle!

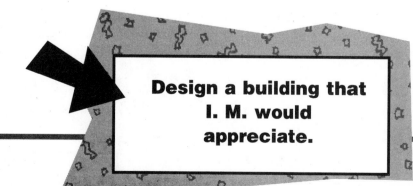

Design a building that I. M. would appreciate.

27

U. S. Grant
1822, Ohio

U. S.'s real initials were H. U. At military school, though, they accidentally got his name mixed up. It was hard to argue with the army, so Hiram U. became Ulysses S.

GRANT

U. S. was a terrible student, but a good general. During the Civil War, he smashed Confederate defenses in the West. Meanwhile, the Union commander in the East wasn't attacking, which disturbed President Lincoln. "If you are not using your army," Lincoln said, "I would like to borrow it for a while." Instead he decided to put U. S. in charge. U. S. did use the army and used it well. Before long the war was over.

If you had to change your name, what would you change it to? Why?

From *Birthday a Day*, published by GoodYearBooks. Copyright © 1996 Stephen Currie.

April

28

Frances Davis
1882, North Carolina

Frances had a difficult childhood. Her father ran off when she was very young, and her mother died soon afterward. Frances lived with mean guardians who hired her out as a servant to make money for themselves. Luckily, one of the families Frances worked for helped her run away and become a nurse.

In 1918, she became the first African American nurse to serve in the American Red Cross. Frances also spent time with children. In fact, the woman who had been to *nursing* school wound up running her own *nursery* school!

Name three qualities that a nurse needs to have. Explain why.

From *Birthday a Day*, published by GoodYearBooks. Copyright © 1996 Stephen Currie.

April
29

Duke Ellington
1899, District of Columbia

The trouble with being a genius is that you lose a lot of sleep. Duke, a pianist and composer best known for writing songs and jazz pieces, once described the life of a composer this way: "You go home expecting to go right to bed. On the way, you pass the piano. . . . When you look up, it's 7:00 A.M."

Duke was not always interested in music. As a child, he had to be made to practice piano. Before becoming a musician, he painted signs and worked at a soda fountain. The name of his first composition? "Soda Fountain Rag."

Duke was really only a nickname. Write how he might have gotten it.

From *Birthday a Day*, published by GoodYearBooks. Copyright © 1996 Stephen Currie.

Karl Gauss

1777, Germany

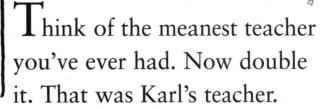

Think of the meanest teacher you've ever had. Now double it. That was Karl's teacher. Once, to punish the class, he made them figure out the sum of all the numbers from 1 to 1,000. Pencils scratched away—except Karl's. He'd found a pattern. 1 + 999 was 1,000. So were 2 + 998, 3 + 997, and so on. In all, there were 499 pairs that added to 1,000, plus the thousand at the end, and the five hundred right in the middle. Multiplying and adding, Karl got 500,500. The whole process took him just a minute or two. He had outfoxed his teacher. You won't be surprised to learn that he went on to become a famous mathematician.

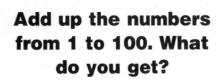

Add up the numbers from 1 to 100. What do you get?

1

Mother Jones

1843, Ireland

"Mother" Mary Jones traveled all over America with scarcely a penny. She seldom carried enough money to buy dinner, let alone a train ticket or a hotel room. How did she do it? Well, Mary was called "Mother" for a reason. When workers needed help, Mother was there: urging them to stand up for their rights, marching to the president's house with child laborers, helping coal miners' wives beat back mine owners with mops and brooms. When she traveled, she knew workers would share everything they had with her—and she was never left in the lurch.

Write a story about Mother Jones from the viewpoint of one of the workers she helped.

From *Birthday a Day*, published by GoodYearBooks. Copyright © 1996 Stephen Currie.

Elijah McCoy
1843, Ontario

THANKS, ELIJAH!

Imagine having to oil your car's engine every evening! Trains used to need that kind of care. Every few hours, the train would stop so the fireman could pour new oil into the engine. When Elijah worked as a fireman, it bothered him to spend so much time and effort on oiling. He used his scientific background to design a new way: a special cup that slowly released oil while the engine was running. The cup was a big success. Elijah went on to invent many more things, including lawn sprinklers and an ironing board.

Combine water and vegetable oil. Write a description or draw a diagram of what happens.

May
3

Golda Meir
1898, Ukraine

Even though Golda wasn't born till 1898, she signed the Declaration of Independence. Of course, it was Israel's Declaration, not that of the United States! Israel did not become an independent country until 1947. Golda was one of the people who made it a nation. For five years, in fact, she was Prime Minister. The new country had several important questions to answer. For instance, which new settlers should be allowed in? Golda had an answer. Since Israel was set up to be a Jewish country, she said, any Jew could move there. She argued so well, her idea became the law.

Write some laws you would need if you were starting a new country.

From *Birthday a Day*, published by GoodYearBooks. Copyright © 1996 Stephen Currie.

May

4

Alice Liddell
1852, England

One hot July day when Alice was a girl, she and her sisters went on a picnic with a man named Charles Dodgson. After lunch, Charles made up a story about a girl who dreamed she fell down a rabbit hole. It must have been a good story. Charles kept pretending to fall asleep, and Alice kept "waking" him by shouting "More! More!" When the day was over, Alice asked for a copy, so Charles wrote it down. He published it under the name of Lewis Carroll. As for Alice, who liked to play croquet and whose fireplace had a huge mirror over it, she was the inspiration for *Alice in Wonderland*.

Plan your own ideal picnic. What will you have?

May
5

Nellie Bly
1867, Pennsylvania

Nellie was an unusually brave reporter. She would do anything to get the story she wanted. Once she wondered how quickly lifeguards could save people, so she threw herself off a boat and acted as if she were drowning. (Luckily, it didn't take long.) Another time, she wanted to know what conditions were like in a mental institution. When no one would let her visit, Nellie pretended to be mentally disturbed and was admitted! She spent a week there before her editors got her out. Thousands of curious people bought newspapers to read all about the poor conditions. But more importantly, her report brought about much needed reforms.

Write your own newspaper article about an unusual situation.

Martin Delany

1812, West Virginia

Doctor, lawyer, soldier, writer, politician—Martin was all of these and more. When a deadly disease struck Pittsburgh, Martin's medical skills helped beat it. Martin wrote books urging African Americans to think about moving to South America. He even explored part of Africa to see if settling there would make sense. During the Civil War, Martin enlisted soldiers to fight for the Union. He also became one of the first African American officers. After the war, Martin helped newly-freed slaves. When he died at age seventy-two, he'd done enough to fill several lifetimes.

List Martin's jobs in the order of their importance. Explain your rating.

Eva Peron
1919, Argentina

Eva was Argentina's First Lady. Many Argentines adored her. People lined up to touch a ballot box because it contained her vote. Men used flowers to spell out her name. Eva was called "La Dama de la Esperanza"—"Lady of Hope."

Popular as she was, though, you were wise to stay on Eva's good side. Things happened to people she didn't like. An actress offended Eva, so Eva banned her movies. When some students coughed during a speech Eva was giving, she had them expelled from college. Imagine what might have happened to someone who used flowers to *mis*spell her name!

> **Use some unusual material to spell Eva's name—properly!**

From *Birthday a Day*, published by GoodYearBooks. Copyright © 1996 Stephen Currie.

Lucretia Blankenburg

1845, Ohio

Lucretia's mother was graduating from medical school. It should have been a great occasion, but the mood was ugly. Many men in town opposed women doctors. Lucretia was both proud and frightened. She never forgot those fears, or her relief when there was no violence. For the rest of her life, Lucretia worked to make the world a place where "great occasions" could stay that way. She married the mayor of Philadelphia and helped plan policies. She hired women police officers, and she started charities to help people in need. Lucretia did so much, many people called her the "co-mayor"!

If you were mayor, what would you do? Write your ideas down.

Belle Boyd

1844, West Virginia

During the Civil War, Belle liked to invite Union officers over for dinner. While they ate, she'd ask them questions: how many soldiers they had, where they would attack next, how strong they thought the Confederate armies were. The officers always told her. Unknown to them, however, Belle was a Confederate spy. The next day, she'd saddle her horse and go tell Southern commanders what she had heard. Getting friendly with Union officers paid off in another way too. Belle wound up marrying one!

Get a friend and act out one of Belle's conversations with an officer.

From *Birthday a Day*, published by GoodYearBooks. Copyright © 1996 Stephen Currie.

Fred Astaire

1899, Nebraska

The first time Fred tried out for a movie, the director judged his work like this: "Can't act, slightly bald, can dance a little." He was wrong. Fred acted, Fred sang, and Fred danced— a lot!

Fred started dance lessons at age four. When he was seven, he and his sister were the stars of a show called "Juvenile Artists Presenting an Electric Musical Toe-Dancing Novelty." Whew! As Fred grew older, his tap dancing talent got him into plays and finally into movies. Show business can be an unfriendly place, but Fred was respected by almost everyone he met.

Write a very complicated name for a simple show.

From *Birthday a Day*, published by GoodYearBooks. Copyright © 1996 Stephen Currie.

Salvador Dali
1904, Spain

Salvador called his paintings "surreal," which means beyond reality. You've seen watches, lions, eggs, and telephones. But have you ever seen a lion with a fried egg in its mouth? A phone suspended in mid-air? A bent watch dangling over the edge of a cliff? Salvador painted everyday objects in unusual combinations. Some people loved his work. Others said he wasted his talent on nonsense. Once Salvador was asked to give a talk about his paintings. He showed up in a deep-sea diving suit, complete with helmet. No one was terribly surprised.

Make your own "surreal" painting.

From *Birthday a Day*, published by GoodYearBooks. Copyright © 1996 Stephen Currie.

Edward Lear

1812, England

Though Edward spent most of his life as a painter, most of his art is forgotten now. Instead, we remember him for the rhymes he used to make up to amuse children. Edward's most famous poem was called "The Owl and the Pussycat." He also wrote verses called "limericks," which go something like this:

Ed had brothers and sisters like mad.
He had more than your mom, or your dad.
All in all, he had plenty:
The total was twenty.
They were nice to him, though; he was glad.

Try writing your own limerick.

May
13

Shipwreck Kelly
1893, New York

Alvin Kelly's nickname came from his years of being a sailor. But he became famous for sitting on flagpoles. He'd climb up one and stay as long as he could. Shipwreck usually built himself a perch barely big enough to sit on. When he slept, he stuck his thumbs into holes on the pole so he wouldn't fall. Thousands of people stopped by to watch. His wife came to visit Shipwreck every Sunday he was in the air. If you add up all of Shipwreck's time on flagpoles, it comes to two and a half years, including forty hours in snowstorms. Shipwreck's record was forty-nine days in a row!

Stand on a piece of paper for as long as you possibly can.

From *Birthday a Day*, published by GoodYearBooks. Copyright © 1996 Stephen Currie.

May 14

Minerva Parker Nichols
1861, Illinois

When Minerva became an architect, her family wasn't surprised. Her grandfather had been one too. Minerva soon learned every detail of her job. One builder said: "She knows not only her business, but mine."

Minerva designed all kinds of buildings, from clubhouses to spaghetti factories. Each building she planned had its own style. Some were like castles from the Middle Ages. Others looked like they belonged in colonial America or the Middle East. Even within a house, Minerva liked to use different designs. After all, she pointed out, rooms are used for different purposes, so why shouldn't they look different too?

Draw a plan for a spaghetti factory.

May 15

Tenzing Norgay
1914, Nepal

It was the tallest mountain in the world. Most people called it "Mount Everest," but Tenzing knew it as "Chomolungma"—"the mountain so high no bird can fly over it." Tenzing could see this mountain from the house where he grew up. He had always dreamed of climbing it. Several times Tenzing went on expeditions that couldn't make it all the way up. Then he joined a climb led by a man named Edmund Hillary. After many hard days of work in cold and stormy weather, Tenzing and Edmund reached the top. They were on the "roof of the world"—the first people to stand so high.

Imagine you were Tenzing. Write what it feels like to be on Mount Everest.

From *Birthday a Day*, published by GoodYearBooks. Copyright © 1996 Stephen Currie.

Elizabeth Peabody

1804, Massachusetts

Elizabeth described kindergarten as "a garden whose plants are human." Just as plants would bloom with plenty of sunshine, water, and soil, she said children would flourish with proper care. To try her ideas she began her own school. In fact, Elizabeth was so interested in children, she often forgot about everything else. She slept in her bonnet, wore her glasses on her chin, and carried an extra toothbrush in her handbag. She'd talk about children to anyone who would listen. And once she had your attention, it was hard to get her to stop!

Name three qualities a kindergarten teacher should have. Why did you choose them?

May 17

Edward Jenner
1749, England

Smallpox was a terrible disease. Many people died from it, and others got scars that never went away. The only good thing about smallpox was you couldn't get it twice.

Milkmaids, though, never even got it once. Why? Edward knew that cows got a similar disease called cowpox. He guessed that the milkmaids were catching cowpox. It didn't make them very sick, but it fooled their bodies into thinking they'd had smallpox instead. So Edward came up with a plan: give people cowpox on purpose! His new "vaccine" worked, and thanks to Edward, smallpox has been wiped out.

Write down all the diseases you can think of.

Bertrand Russell
1872, England

If a sentence is false, then its opposite must be—

Did you say "true"?

Then try these:

This sentence has four Ts.

This sentence has three Ts.

This sentence does not have four Ts.

Oops! They're all false. Sentences like these are called "paradoxes." They can make your brain spin. Bertrand was a reporter, scientist, and peace worker, but we remember him best for studying paradoxes. His most famous book on math and logic went on for nearly two thousand pages! And if Bertrand had been given two medical degrees, would he be a "pair-o'-docs"?

Fix those sentences so they are true.

May
19

Malcolm X
1925, Nebraska

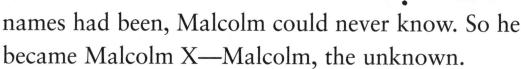

In math, "x" stands for the unknown. Malcolm was born Malcolm Little. "Little" was the name slave owners had given his ancestors. What their real names had been, Malcolm could never know. So he became Malcolm X—Malcolm, the unknown.

Malcolm was a leader in the struggle for African Americans' rights. He did not always agree with other leaders, though. Malcolm felt that African Americans should get their rights any way they could—even by violence. His enemies said he was full of anger and hate. His friends said he was full of love and respect. As for Malcolm, he knew they were both right!

Ask a relative where your ancestors came from. Find those places on a map.

From *Birthday a Day*, published by GoodYearBooks. Copyright © 1996 Stephen Currie.

May 20

John Stuart Mill
1806, England

Do you get too much homework?

Don't complain. John's father thought he could teach his son anything, as long as he did it early enough. At age three, John could read and write—in ancient Greek. Before he was ten, Mr. Mill had him doing college work. Sadly, though, work was all John did. He had no friends. Walking was his only exercise, and Mr. Mill always came along to quiz him. You won't be surprised to learn that John became a great thinker. But you probably won't be surprised, either, to learn that he had a nervous breakdown when he was just twenty years old.

Make up quiz questions you can answer. Try them on a friend.

May
21

Frances Densmore
1867, Minnesota

Most recording studios have soundproof walls, acoustic tiles, and high-tech equipment. Not Frances's. She recorded in coal sheds, medical tents, and even jail cells!

Frances had studied music for years. She worked as a teacher, a choir director, and an organist. Then she grew interested in Native American music and visited villages to record songs on tape. Travel wasn't easy. If villages could only be reached by canoe, Frances paddled to them, a huge tape recorder beside her. Even at age eighty-seven, Frances was still tracking down musicians in Florida.

➡️ **Ask someone to sing a song they learned from someone else. If you can, record it.**

From *Birthday a Day*, published by GoodYearBooks. Copyright © 1996 Stephen Currie.

Mary Cassatt

1844, Pennsylvania

When an artist named Edgar Degas saw one of Mary's paintings, he was astonished. "I will not admit that a woman can paint like that!" he said. But as Mary painted one beautiful portrait after another, he changed his mind. Clearly, a woman *could* paint like that.

Mary became a painter even though her father thought it was a terrible idea. She studied in France, where there was a group of artists she admired. Winning their approval was hard, but she did it. She even won her family's approval. They came to live with her in France, and they often served as her models.

Sketch a portrait of a friend.

Carl von Linne

1707, Sweden

Are bats and sparrows related?

Even though they both fly, you probably said "no." That's because you used Carl's system. Carl spent his life figuring out which animals and plants were related. To make his groups, he paid lots of attention to bones and skin covering, but not much to color. Each animal got two scientific names. Animals that are closely related have the same first name: can you identify "felis tigris," "felis leo," and "felis domesticus"? Animals that aren't related have names that are different from each other. Carl's system worked so well, we still use it today.

Make up your own animal. How is it related to other animals?

Lillian Gilbreth
1878, California

Tired, cranky people don't get much work done. Lillian and her husband watched people at work, and they saw plenty of tired, cranky people. There were cooks who ran all day because their equipment was too far apart, and office workers with sore backs from using the wrong size desks. When Lillian built them new kitchens and adjustable tables, people got more done. Lillian had another job too: raising twelve children. The kids knew all about not wasting time. They buttoned their shirts from the bottom up because their parents said it was faster. They even had their tonsils taken out in record time!

Make something out of paper. Now see if you can do it in fewer steps.

May
25

Dorothea Lange
1895, New Jersey

During the Great Depression of the 1930s, millions of people were out of work. Dorothea was lucky. She was a photographer, and she had a job. But she worried about people who didn't. One morning, she saw a woman sitting in a field with her children. They were dirty and cold. The mother told Dorothea that they'd scarcely eaten for days. To buy food, they'd had to sell the tires off their car. Dorothea asked to take their picture. The woman agreed. The published photograph, "Migrant Mother," got the government to give extra help to many Americans who really needed it.

Draw what you think "Migrant Mother" might have looked like.

From *Birthday a Day*, published by GoodYearBooks. Copyright © 1996 Stephen Currie.

Sally Ride
1951, California

When the seventh space shuttle mission took off in 1983, hundreds of thousands of people came to watch. Many wore T-shirts that said "Ride, Sally Ride." They were there to cheer on Sally—the first American woman in space.

Sally got to be an astronaut by being an outstanding scientist. For the space shuttle, she designed a mechanical "arm" that could send out satellites and catch them again. As a girl, Sally liked both tennis and science. The "arm" combined the two. It worked very much like a gigantic tennis racquet!

Build a contraption that can pick things up off the floor.

Rachel Carson
1907, Pennsylvania

Farmers usually try to kill bugs that destroy crops. But when they used a bug poison, or pesticide, called DDT, it was a disaster. DDT wouldn't go away. Birds ate poisoned bugs and built up DDT in their own systems. DDT got into water and poisoned fish. Soon the mammals that ate birds and fish were in danger.

Rachel was a biologist who studied this problem. She had already written several books about wildlife and the oceans, so she wrote a book about DDT too. She called it *Silent Spring*. The book made people think about the world around them—and helped get DDT banned.

Get some water from a pond or river. Look at it under a microscope. Draw what you see.

May
28

The Dionne Quintuplets
1934, Ontario

A typical baby born these days might weigh seven or eight pounds. That's almost as much as all five Dionne sisters weighed at birth—put together!

Just by being born, Emilie, Cecile, Yvonne, Marie, and Annette made headlines. A set of quintuplets had never survived before. The girls became a tourist attraction. People sold Dionne lampshades, Dionne bars of soap, quintuplet souvenir pencils. Doctors begged to be allowed to study them. Although the girls looked alike, their personalities were different. Even at age four, no two of them had the same favorite color!

Find some objects that weigh about as much as an average baby.

May

29

Patrick Henry
1736, Virginia

The Declaration of Independence said that the U.S. would be a separate country. The Constitution set up the way the country would be run. Many people who liked the Declaration weren't so sure about the Constitution. Like Patrick. He felt so strongly about independence that he once said "Give me liberty, or give me death!" But Patrick felt that the Constitution wouldn't protect people's rights very well. It didn't guarantee that people could say what they thought, for instance, or follow the religion they liked. So Patrick helped add a section to protect freedoms like these. The new section's name? The "Bill of Rights."

Which do you think was more important—the Declaration or the Constitution? Why?

From *Birthday a Day*, published by GoodYearBooks. Copyright © 1996 Stephen Currie.

Dorothy Eustis

1886, Pennsylvania

Dorothy trained German shepherds for armies and police forces. While studying dog training methods, she found a school in Europe that trained dogs to guide blind people. She wrote an article about the dogs. A few months later, a blind salesman wrote to ask for help in getting a guide dog like the ones in her article. Dorothy decided to train one herself. Soon she was flooded with requests for guide dogs. Using money she had inherited, she founded a school called The Seeing Eye. Even after her death, Dorothy's school continued to train "Seeing Eye" dogs.

Close your eyes. Get a friend to guide you through an obstacle course.

May
31

John Ringling
1866, Iowa

For six years John and his brothers ran the Classic Concert Company. They put on a good show. John danced and clowned. The others juggled and played music. They even had a dancing bear and a trained horse. But they didn't have an elephant, and elephants were what their audiences wanted to see. So the brothers bought one, and the money came rolling in. Now the brothers performed all over the country. They gave up traveling in wagons and took the train instead. Oh, yes, they changed their name too—to the Ringling Brothers Circus. It just goes to show what buying an elephant can do!

Plan your own circus. What acts will you have?

From *Birthday a Day*, published by GoodYearBooks. Copyright © 1996 Stephen Currie.

Jacques Marquette

1637, France

Jacques was a missionary among the North American Indians. He lived with them and learned to speak their languages. He learned so well, he was asked to join an explorer named Louis Jolliet on a journey to Lake Michigan and the Mississippi River. Jacques and Louis took five men and two bark canoes. When they couldn't paddle, they walked, carrying the boats. Jacques kept a journal of this trip. How well is it remembered today? Well, not far from Lake Michigan, you can find Marquette University, Marquette Park, the Marquette River, and Marquette Island—not to mention roads, counties, and towns named after Jacques!

Find out more about Marquette. Trace his journey on a map.

From *Birthday a Day* published by GoodYearBooks. Copyright © 1996 Stephen Currie.

June 2

Hedda Hopper
1890, *Pennsylvania*

Psst! Wanna hear a story? An actor named DeWolf Hopper got married six times. Three of his wives were named Ida, Edna, and Nella. (Say that five times, real fast.) When he fell in love with Elda Furry, he made her change her first name so it wouldn't sound so much like his other wives. She did, and that's how she became Hedda Hopper. Hedda was an actress and a radio broadcaster. But she was best known for writing a gossip column. If you wanted to know which movie stars didn't get along, or what actor was getting married, Hedda was the person to ask. Got that? Good! Pass it on.

Would you want your name in Hedda's column? Why or why not?

From *Birthday a Day*, published by GoodYearBooks. Copyright © 1996 Stephen Currie.

From *Birthday a Day*, published by GoodYearBooks. Copyright © 1996 Stephen Currie.

June
3

Charles Drew
1904, District of Columbia

Everybody's blood belongs to one of four groups: A, B, AB, or O. If you lost lots of blood and needed more, a hospital would give you some of your type. But during World War II, most doctors sorted blood by race as well as by type. African Americans with "O" blood, say, could only get "O" blood from other African Americans. Charles was a scientist who said this system was crazy. He knew what he was talking about. He had studied blood and figured out ways of keeping it fresh. But no one listened. In 1950, Charles died after a car crash—when a "whites-only" hospital wouldn't give him the blood he needed.

Find your pulse. Use a watch to time it. How many times a minute does your heart beat?

George the Third
1738, England

George liked being king of England, and he took his job seriously. But when some of his subjects challenged his ideas, George treated them like naughty children. When they complained, he punished them instead of listening. As the complaints got louder, the punishments got fiercer: taxes, threats, and finally war. George thought the rebels would lose right away and apologize. He was wrong. That war was the American Revolution. We remember Washington's, Franklin's, and Jefferson's contributions toward America's independence. But George the Third might have done more than anyone else!

Write a polite letter of complaint from the colonists to George.

From *Birthday a Day*, published by GoodYearBooks. Copyright © 1996 Stephen Currie.

Pancho Villa
1878, Mexico

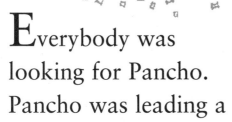Everybody was looking for Pancho. Pancho was leading a revolt in the northern part of Mexico, so the Mexican government was looking for him. He had gone on raids into the United States, so the U.S. was looking for him too. He was on the side of Mexico's poorest people, so the rich were looking for him as well. Unfortunately for them, Pancho was hard to find. He ran most of northern Mexico from hideouts in the hills. He and his men robbed trains and stagecoaches. Pancho even printed his own money. When armies came near, he hid or attacked them first—and usually won!

> **Think of the best hiding place you know. Draw a map showing how to get there.**

The Dalai Lama

1935, China

Tibetans believe in "reincarnation"—coming back to life after death. When the Tibetan priest called the Dalai Lama died in 1933, a group of priests went looking for a child who might be his reincarnation. They found a two-year-old named Tanchu whose head was about the right shape. When they showed Tanchu a handful of objects, he clinched it by picking up the ones that had belonged to the former Dalai Lama. But by the time Tanchu was an adult, China had taken over Tibet, and was trying to eliminate Tibetan ways. What did Tanchu do then? He moved to India and continued to lead his people.

Display three things that are yours and three that aren't. Can a friend tell which is yours?

From *Birthday a Day*, published by GoodYearBooks. Copyright © 1996 Stephen Currie.

Virginia Apgar
1909, New Jersey

How old were you the first time you got a grade? Younger than you think.

Virginia was a doctor. She noticed that most doctors didn't pay much attention to newborn babies. They were too worried about the mother. Sometimes the babies were born with problems—but no one was watching. So Virginia developed a scoring system. Babies with good breathing, heartbeats, and reflexes scored 10. Less healthy babies scored lower. With a low enough score, babies went right to a special nursery. Almost all babies get an "Apgar" score now—probably including you!

Invent your own scoring system for something. Explain it.

June 8

Frank Lloyd Wright
1869, Wisconsin

How would you like to have a waterfall in your living room?

Frank designed buildings. He liked to bring the outside in and take the inside out. He was known for courtyards, balconies, and windows that curved around trees. Most of his buildings were long and low. Roofs jutted out way past the outside walls, and rooms flowed into each other through wide doorways. Frank wanted his buildings to fit into the landscape. He liked to build on hillsides, and he used earth colors to paint his houses. And as for the waterfall: one of his most famous houses is built right on top of one.

Design a building that Frank would appreciate.

From *Birthday a Day*, published by GoodYearBooks. Copyright © 1996 Stephen Currie.

9

Gertrude Muller

1887, Indiana

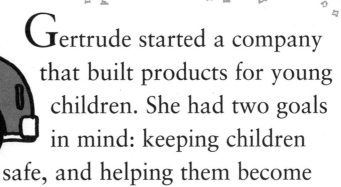

Gertrude started a company that built products for young children. She had two goals in mind: keeping children safe, and helping them become independent. If you have younger brothers or sisters, you know how often they need you to get things from high shelves—and how often they climb up themselves! Gertrude sold folding steps that let children get up safely and without help. Her "comfy-safe" car seat let kids ride high enough to see out the car window. But mostly, it protected them in accidents. Today, car seats save many small children's lives every year. Gertrude would be proud.

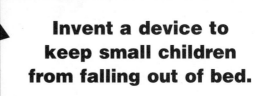

Invent a device to keep small children from falling out of bed.

From *Birthday a Day*, published by GoodYearBooks. Copyright © 1996 Stephen Currie.

Judy Garland

1922, Minnesota

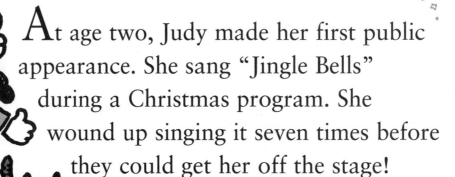

At age two, Judy made her first public appearance. She sang "Jingle Bells" during a Christmas program. She wound up singing it seven times before they could get her off the stage! While still a child, Judy became a professional singer. Soon she was appearing in movies. You've probably seen her in her most famous role: Dorothy in *The Wizard of Oz*. She almost wasn't cast as Dorothy, though. An actress named Shirley Temple was the studio's first choice, but Shirley wasn't available. It was just as well though. Judy was made for the part. Her favorite color was green—the color of the Emerald City.

What movie role would you most want to play? Why?

From *Birthday a Day*, published by GoodYearBooks. Copyright © 1996 Stephen Currie.

From *Birthday a Day*, published by GoodYearBooks. Copyright © 1996 Stephen Currie.

June
11

Jacques Cousteau
1910, France

An astronaut travels into outer space. What do you suppose an "oceanaut" does?

Jacques was one of the first people to travel deep into the world's oceans. He invented equipment that allowed divers to explore far below the surface. He designed underwater buildings, like space stations, where people could live for weeks at a time. He also made about a hundred movies about his adventures. These films showed the sunken ships, the strange wildlife, and the amazing caves Jacques found beneath the sea. When he worked, Jacques usually wore diving gear. He did own one tie—but he saved it for his dinners with presidents!

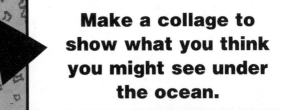

Make a collage to show what you think you might see under the ocean.

12

Anne Frank
1929, Germany

When Anne started a diary, she thought no one would be interested in it. Sadly, she was wrong.

In 1942, Anne's family went into hiding. Nazi soldiers had come to her home in Holland. They meant to get rid of all Jews, including Anne. For two years the Franks hid in a tiny attic. They couldn't go out or speak above a whisper; they scarcely dared to look through the curtains. During this time Anne kept a journal. She wrote down her longings for freedom and friends. Then Anne's hiding place was found. She was killed, but her diary survived: a monument to a teenager whose only "crime" was her religion.

Draw or build what you think Anne's attic looked like.

From *Birthday a Day*, published by GoodYearBooks. Copyright © 1996 Stephen Currie.

June
13

Luis Alvarez
1911, California

What happened to the dinosaurs?

No one knows for sure. But Luis had a guess. Working with his son, he found a metal called "iridium" in a layer of soil. Iridium is rare on earth, but it's common in meteorites. The soil dated to the time of the last dinosaurs. Did dinosaurs die out because a meteorite crashed into the Earth? Luis thought so. Many scientists thought Luis's idea sounded bizarre at first. Luckily, Luis was used to criticism. When he had studied radar and nuclear energy, he was known as "the wild idea man." A few of those wild ideas turned out to be right!

Draw three kinds of dinosaurs. Estimate how much they weigh. Check your answers.

June
14

Harriet Beecher Stowe
1811, Connecticut

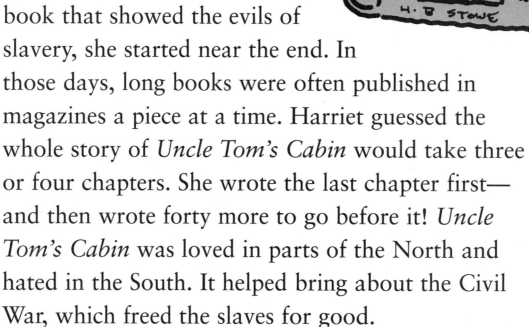

When you write a story, you probably begin at the beginning. But when Harriet wrote *Uncle Tom's Cabin*, a book that showed the evils of slavery, she started near the end. In those days, long books were often published in magazines a piece at a time. Harriet guessed the whole story of *Uncle Tom's Cabin* would take three or four chapters. She wrote the last chapter first—and then wrote forty more to go before it! *Uncle Tom's Cabin* was loved in parts of the North and hated in the South. It helped bring about the Civil War, which freed the slaves for good.

Write the last sentence of a story. Have a friend write the rest.

From *Birthday a Day*, published by GoodYearBooks. Copyright © 1996 Stephen Currie.

June

15

Issa
1763, Japan

Issa wrote haikus.
Haikus are three-line poems.
Count the syllables!
   The first line has five.
   The second must have seven.
   The third, five again.
      Issa's life was hard.
      He hated his stepmother.
      His children died young.
         But he could write well.
         His haikus have a lot of
         Animals and jokes.
            Issa was a name
            He only used for writing.
            It means "cup of tea."

Write your own haiku.

Mary Katherine Goddard

1738, Connecticut

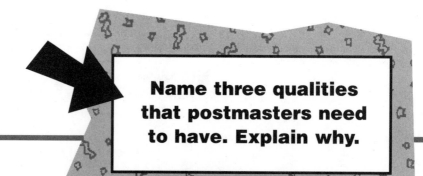

Publisher, printer, and postmaster—Mary Katherine was all three. She printed newspapers in Pennsylvania, Rhode Island, and Maryland. She also published books. The Pennsylvania print shop, where she and her brother worked together, was one of the largest in the colonies. Later on, Mary Katherine took charge of the postal service in Baltimore. She did an excellent job for fourteen years. When she was replaced, two hundred businessmen signed a petition asking that she be kept on the job!

Name three qualities that postmasters need to have. Explain why.

From *Birthday a Day*, published by GoodYearBooks. Copyright © 1996 Stephen Currie.

17

M. C. Escher

1898, The Netherlands

A hand is drawing a picture of a hand. But look closely. The hand that's being drawn has a pencil too. In fact, it's drawing the first hand.

Welcome to the world of M. C. Escher. M. C. once wanted to be an architect, but he gave it up for drawing. Imagine being on a staircase that takes you up, up, up—and back to where you started without going down. Impossible? M. C. drew it. He also drew "tessellations." Try covering a table with blocks all the same shape and size. Don't leave any spaces. It's easy with squares or certain kinds of triangles. But M. C. did it with blocks shaped like bulldogs, lizards, and beetles!

Find as many shapes as you can that "tessellate."

June
18

Anastasia Romanov
1901, Russia

Anastasia's father was named Nicholas, but her family wasn't nickel-less at all. They ruled Russia, and they had lots of money. They had five hundred cars and thirty thousand servants. Their jewel collection was dazzling. Part of this fortune belonged to Anastasia. But many Russians were tired of being poor while their leaders were so rich. They set up their own government and killed the Romanov family. Or did they? Some say that Anastasia escaped. Many women have claimed to be the long-lost princess. Look carefully at the next woman you meet—she just might be related to royalty!

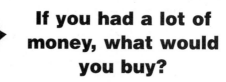

If you had a lot of money, what would you buy?

From *Birthday a Day*, published by GoodYearBooks. Copyright © 1996 Stephen Currie.

Aung San Suu Kyi

1945, Myanmar

Would you rather go live in a poor country, ruled by a dictator, where you might be put in jail? Or would you rather go home?

Suu Kyi did both. Though she left Myanmar as a girl, she felt that she needed to help the people of her country. So she went back. For nearly a year she worked for democracy. But working for democracy was against the law. Suu Kyi was arrested. The government offered to free her if she would leave the country. Suu Kyi refused. The world did not forget her, though. For her efforts, she was given the Nobel Peace Prize.

Would you have chosen to leave the country so you could be free?

June 20

Helen Miller Gould
1868, New York

Helen had tons of money—and she gave most of it away.

Helen's father was a wealthy businessman. He lived in luxury and loved to be the center of attention. Helen didn't. When she inherited his fortune, she gave most of it to hospitals, food banks, and the poor. Each year, about three-fourths of her income went to charity. Helen tried to respond to every appeal for help she could. Once she bought two new beds for a children's hospital. She had only one request: that the beds be given to the two least interesting children they had—the children no one else would bother to help!

If you had lots of money, what charity would you give it to? Explain your choice.

From *Birthday a Day*, published by GoodYearBooks. Copyright © 1996 Stephen Currie.

Henry Tanner

1859, Pennsylvania

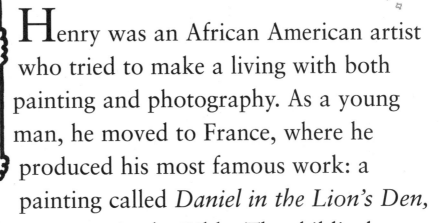

Henry was an African American artist who tried to make a living with both painting and photography. As a young man, he moved to France, where he produced his most famous work: a painting called *Daniel in the Lion's Den*, based on a story in the Bible. That biblical picture was so popular, Henry decided to do more. A businessman who saw Henry's picture gave Henry money to travel in the Middle East, so he could see firsthand what the landscapes looked like. For the next twenty years, Henry won prizes for his paintings of biblical scenes, and he became an inspiration to young artists around the world.

How many types of art can you think of? Make a list.

June
22

John Dillinger
1903, Indiana

Most criminals stay away from the police. Not John. Besides robbing factories and banks, he raided two police stations. Each time he came away loaded with machine guns and bulletproof vests. Even when John was captured, he didn't spend much time in jail. Once his gang burst into the prison and freed him. Another time, John whittled a fake gun from a

piece of wood. Locking up the sheriff, he escaped in a police car! But John couldn't keep going forever. As he left a theater one night, "Public Enemy Number One" was shot and killed by the FBI. His luck had finally run out.

Make up another dramatic escape for John. Draw a diagram.

From *Birthday a Day*, published by GoodYearBooks. Copyright © 1996 Stephen Currie.

23

Wilma Rudolph

1940, Tennessee

By the time Wilma was four, she'd had pneumonia twice and scarlet fever twice more. Polio had made her left leg so weak she couldn't use it. How do you think she became famous?

Little by little, heat and water treatments strengthened Wilma's leg. Family members massaged it four times a day. The work paid off. Wilma took up basketball, then track. In college, she moved so slowly she was usually late for class, but she ran hard during races! At the 1960 Olympics, Wilma won three gold medals in running. Quite an achievement for a girl who once could barely walk.

Think of words that mean the same as *fast*. Use those words in a poem.

From *Birthday a Day*, published by GoodYearBooks. Copyright © 1996 Stephen Currie.

Gustavus Swift

1839, Massachusetts

People in big Eastern cities ate plenty of beef, but getting it to them was hard. Usually companies shipped cattle by train from Chicago. That was expensive. Gustavus decided to slaughter the cattle in Chicago and send just the beef in a special refrigerated railroad car. Everyone thought he was crazy. His business partner wanted nothing to do with it. Neither did most railroads. In the end, Gustavus sank his own money into the project. It worked, and Gustavus became a famous meat packer. But perhaps we could have guessed he'd be in the food business: he was born in a town called Sandwich!

Look on a map. Find three other towns with names that are related to food.

From *Birthday a Day*, published by GoodYearBooks. Copyright © 1996 Stephen Currie.

25

Rose O'Neill
1874, *Pennsylvania*

Kewpies were cute little creatures with wings and topknots, and they brought Rose, their creator, more than a million dollars. Rose drew Kewpies and wrote books about them. She designed a Kewpie doll, which was incredibly popular: a little like Barbie, Smurfs, and Ninja Turtles, all rolled into one. Every time someone bought a Kewpie doll, necktie, salt shaker, or bar of soap, Rose made money. She built herself a mansion, which she named after a fairy tale character. She used baby talk whenever she felt like it, and she called her hot water heater—what else?—"Kewpie."

Design a doll. Write an advertisement for it.

Babe Didrikson Zaharias

1912, Texas

When Babe decided to take up golf, many people asked her why. She replied: "I'd done everything else."

She had too. As a teenager, Babe joined a sports club. In two years she won ninety-two medals. At a national track championship she finished first. Second place went to a 22-member team! Besides track, Babe was a champion at swimming, figure skating, basketball, and many other sports. She once won six golf tournaments in six weeks. The only sport she tried without mastering was Ping-Pong. Babe even played the harmonica on the radio and won prizes for designing sports clothes!

Take a survey. Ask people what sports they're best at, and make a graph.

From *Birthday a Day*, published by GoodYearBooks. Copyright © 1996 Stephen Currie.

June 27

Antoinette Perry
1888, Colorado

Aunt Mildred and Uncle George were actors. Whenever Antoinette had a school vacation, she toured with them. They taught her all about the theater. Aunt Mildred got Antoinette her first stage role too. But Antoinette didn't stick with acting. Much as she enjoyed it, she liked directing even better. She loved to think about all the parts of the play: how the scenery would match the dancing, which actors would fit which roles, what the mood should be for each scene. She became a famous director. The "Tony" awards for best American plays are given in her honor.

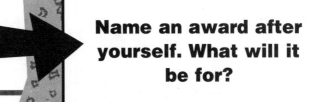

Name an award after yourself. What will it be for?

June 28

Henry the Eighth
1491, England

Getting married to Henry was not a good idea. He went through wives the way allergic people go through tissues: very quickly! While Henry was King of England, he married six different women. He divorced two of them. He even started his own church when the Roman Catholic Pope wouldn't let him divorce the first one. Two other wives weren't so lucky. He had them beheaded. Another wife got sick on her own and died. As for the sixth, she outlived him, which must have been a great relief to her. Surprisingly, Henry's six wives had a total of only three names. Two were called Anne, and three more were named Catherine!

> **Make up a rhyme about Henry and his wives.**

From *Birthday a Day*, published by GoodYearBooks. Copyright © 1996 Stephen Currie.

George Goethals

1858, New York

When the Panama Canal was being dug, George was the man in charge. George was an engineer. He knew all about rivers, currents, dams, and locks. But George needed to know much more for this project. He had to provide food, housing, health care, and entertainment for thirty thousand workers and their families too. George built schools, offices, and gyms. More than that, he paid attention to his workers and their problems. George set aside every Sunday morning for listening to complaints! By the end of the project, even his enemies had to admit he'd done a good job.

Use water and clay to dig your own miniature canal.

From *Birthday a Day*, published by GoodYearBooks. Copyright © 1996 Stephen Currie.

June 30

Lena Horne
1917, New York

Early in Lena's career as a singer and actress, she appeared in a movie called *Stormy Weather*. In the movie Lena sang a song with the same name. The song became her trademark. Wherever she sang, audiences asked for it. "Stormy Weather" also fit parts of Lena's life. As a child, she often had to move from one relative's house to another. "I never let myself love anybody," she said later, "because I knew I couldn't stay around." Audience members also made Lena's life a little stormier than she liked. Once Lena got off the stage to throw plates and a lamp at a person who insulted her!

What muscles do you need most to sing? Explain why you chose them.

From *Birthday a Day*, published by GoodYearBooks. Copyright © 1996 Stephen Currie.

Isaac Sears

1730, Massachusetts

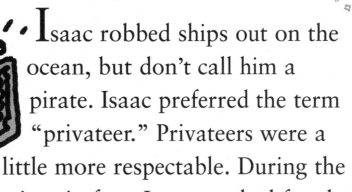

Isaac robbed ships out on the ocean, but don't call him a pirate. Isaac preferred the term "privateer." Privateers were a little more respectable. During the Revolution, in fact, Isaac worked for the American government. He only raided British ships, leaving American ones alone. He worked for American independence on land too. And unlike most pirates, Isaac was a responsible merchant when wars weren't going on. Isaac never buried treasure or owned a parrot that said "Pieces of eight!" But he raided enough ships to make any "real" pirate proud.

Build a clay pirate ship. Test it in water. Will it float?

Thurgood Marshall
1908, Maryland

When Thurgood misbehaved in school, he was forced to read the Constitution over and over. That punishment didn't stop Thurgood from acting up, but it did give him a good understanding of the law! Thurgood went on to become a lawyer. He worked on civil rights cases. Should African American and white children go to the same schools? "Yes," said Thurgood. Should African Americans be allowed to vote or eat in restaurants? "Of course they should," said Thurgood. He argued these cases in the Supreme Court—and won. Not long after that, Thurgood became a Supreme Court Justice himself, the Court's very first African American.

Name three qualities a judge needs to have. Why do you think so?

From *Birthday a Day*, published by GoodYearBooks. Copyright © 1996 Stephen Currie.

July

3

Maria Martin

1796, South Carolina

Maria spent most of her time at her sister Harriet's house. Harriet wasn't healthy, so Maria wound up sewing, paying bills, nursing Harriet, and—oh yes—taking care of Harriet's fourteen children. When she had time, she painted pictures of birds, trees, and insects. An artist and naturalist named John James Audubon saw her work and admired it. He asked her to paint some backgrounds for a series of bird pictures he was painting. Maria did, using her garden for a model. John was thrilled with her "superior talents." He used her backgrounds in his work—and named a woodpecker after her.

Paint a background. Get a friend to put an animal in the picture.

July

4

Rube Goldberg
1883, California

Rube became famous for sketching incredibly complicated machines that did very simple tasks. In Rube's world, everything was connected. Levers, pulleys, animals, and ordinary objects combined to do surprising things. A machine to remove hats involved an alligator, a bowling ball, and a pair of scissors. Want to cool your soup? Scare a cat by dropping dishes. It will run down a fence to pant, exhausted, over your bowl. People expected Rube to behave like his inventions. They were always disappointed to find that he looked perfectly normal and didn't even hang from the chandeliers.

Design your own "Rube Goldberg" machine. Build it, if you can!

From *Birthday a Day*, published by GoodYearBooks. Copyright © 1996 Stephen Currie.

5

P. T. Barnum

1810, Connecticut

"There's a sucker born every minute," P. T. used to say. P. T. believed that people liked to be fooled—if they were fooled in a clever way. P. T. ran museums and circuses. Once he advertised he had a mermaid. He didn't, of course, but thousands of people bought tickets, just to make sure. Another time he displayed a woman he said was 164 years old. It was such fun figuring out how old she really was, no one much minded that he was making it up. Later he said she was really a robot. Guess what? Many people who had already seen her paid to check her out again!

Design a poster for P. T.'s museum. What will it advertise?

July

6

Frida Kahlo
1907, Mexico

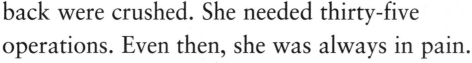

Some people say that suffering can make people great artists. If it does, Frida must have been one of the finest painters ever. At the age of 15, Frida was in a terrible car crash. Her foot and back were crushed. She needed thirty-five operations. Even then, she was always in pain.

Most of Frida's paintings were self-portraits. She used rich and beautiful colors. Though they were lovely at first glance, Frida's paintings could be disturbing up close. Her art often reflected the pain she felt. No wonder someone once said her work was like "a ribbon around a bomb."

Use a mirror to help draw a self-portrait.

From *Birthday a Day*, published by GoodYearBooks. Copyright © 1996 Stephen Currie.

Mariano Vallejo

1808, California

Though California is in the U.S., it once belonged to Mexico. If not for Mariano, it might still. A soldier and a politician, Mariano hated the Mexican government and hoped for independence. When it became clear that independence wasn't a choice, Mariano decided to work with the U.S. instead. He encouraged American settlers to come to California and helped it become a new state. Sadly, he was not rewarded for his work. He spent two months in jail and lost most of his land. But even today, California rings with old Mexican names: San Diego, San Jose, Sacramento—and a city called Vallejo.

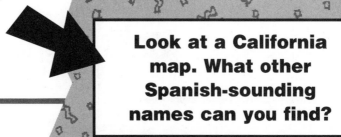

Look at a California map. What other Spanish-sounding names can you find?

July

8

Raffi
1948, Egypt

Raffi Cavoukian wanted to be a folk singer. He learned to play the guitar and memorized the words to dozens of songs. But there were so many other folk singers around, Raffi had a hard time being noticed. Then one day he did a concert just for children. He had a blast. So did his audience. Soon Raffi was recording songs just for kids. Many of the songs he performed were ones he'd written himself. Others were old folk songs. Raffi especially liked songs from different cultures—which makes sense for a boy who moved from Egypt to Canada at the age of ten!

Make up a song that children would like. Tape it.

From *Birthday a Day*, published by GoodYearBooks. Copyright © 1996 Stephen Currie.

July

9

Elizabeth Boit

1849, Massachusetts

To run a business properly, it helps to know math—unless you're as clever as Elizabeth.

Despite being terrible at math, she was a brilliant businesswoman. As a teenager, she worked in a knitting factory. Later she opened her own factory, which specialized in making underwear. Elizabeth expanded her factory whenever she could. At first the factory produced 240 pairs a day. Soon it was 24,000! Elizabeth cared about her 850 workers too. When it rained, she rented streetcars to take them to and from work. It was said that Elizabeth was the smartest person in her town.

What would be your ideal way of getting to work or school? Draw it.

Mary McLeod Bethune

1875, South Carolina

SCHOOL 5 MILES

Mary was an excellent student, even though getting to school was a five-mile walk each day. Her dream was to start a school for African American children. Once she asked a rich man for money to fund it. "Where is the school?" he asked. "It is in my mind and in my soul," Mary replied. That was the right answer; she got the money. The only land she could afford was an old garbage dump, but it was better than nothing. Soon Mary had 250 students. Word spread, and before long presidents were asking Mary's advice. In her will, Mary left the world love, hope, and "a thirst for education."

What would you leave to the world? Write or draw it.

From *Birthday a Day*, published by GoodYearBooks. Copyright © 1996 Stephen Currie.

E. B. White

1899, New York

Y ou probably know E. B.'s children's books: *Charlotte's Web, Stuart Little,* and *The Trumpet of the Swan.* But E. B. wrote much more. He wrote poems, stories, newspaper articles, and ads; he wrote about radios, politics, silly people, and airplanes. E. B. got the writing bug early. As a boy, he borrowed his older brother's typewriter whenever he could. Even after he "retired" to the countryside, he continued to write. You won't be surprised to learn that E. B. kept a few farm animals around his house and perhaps an occasional spider as well.

Make up a story about a farm.

July

12

George Washington Carver

1861, Missouri

Plant cotton one year, peanuts the next. That combination helped keep soil fresh and rich. The cotton could be made into clothes—but the peanuts were of little value until George went to work. A gifted scientist, George had spent his childhood studying plants and flowers in the woods. He soon developed several hundred uses for peanuts, including peanut coffee, peanut soap, vinegar, cheese, and makeup. Could you use peanut ink? George invented that too.

Thanks to George, farmers in the South could keep their soil rich, and make money at the same time.

Open a peanut shell. Look closely at the peanut and the shell. Draw what you see.

From *Birthday a Day*, published by GoodYearBooks. Copyright © 1996 Stephen Currie.

Julius Caesar

100 B.C., Italy

Julius was a general in the Roman army. He won so many battles, from Egypt to Great Britain, that he soon became emperor. Julius enjoyed it a lot. He put up statues of himself in the temples. He put his picture on coins. He even renamed the month "Quintilis" to "July," after himself. Unfortunately for Julius, not everyone approved. He was murdered by friends who thought he was getting too powerful. They tore down the statues—but they didn't change July back to Quintilis. Just as well. Imagine celebrating Independence Day on the "Fourth of Quintilis"!

Make up your own calendar. Give your months interesting names.

Woody Guthrie
1912, Oklahoma

Many Americans thought Woody was as important to the country as Yellowstone National Park. A singer and guitar player, Woody wrote over a thousand songs, including "This Land Is Your Land." Woody sang everywhere: in bars and barber-shops, at work camps and concert halls.

Woody's voice was not beautiful, but he liked it that way. His goal was to match the sounds of America in his music. He said he wanted to sound like "the cab drivers cursing, the cowhands whooping, and the lone wolf barking," and according to most listeners, he did.

Make the sound of "the lone wolf barking." Record it.

From *Birthday a Day*, published by GoodYearBooks. Copyright © 1996 Stephen Currie.

15

Rembrandt Van Rijn

1606, The Netherlands

There's nothing worse than going out of style. Just ask Rembrandt.

Rembrandt began his art career by painting portraits of people he knew. His work was known for its use of light and shadow. The light is often so vivid, you almost expect to see a light bulb glowing in the corner of his paintings! As a young man, Rembrandt had a great reputation. But as he got older, styles changed. No one bought his work, and he died in poverty. For two hundred years, Rembrandt's name was nearly forgotten. Now styles have changed again—and Rembrandt is popular once more.

Paint a picture. Try to get a real contrast between light and dark.

Ida Wells

1862, Mississippi

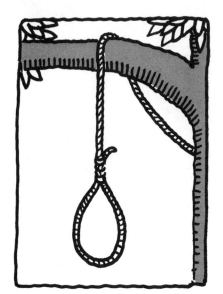

Building a store. Quarreling. Looking people in the eye. These may not seem like terrible crimes to you, but African American men in the South once risked death by doing them. Angry mobs of racists often hanged, or "lynched," African Americans who did things they didn't like. To make things worse, the racists were not punished.

When three men Ida knew were lynched, Ida began to study lynching. She found that more than one hundred men were lynched every year. Worse, most of the victims had not even committed a crime. Over many years, Ida's work helped convince people that lynching was murder.

Think of a time when you were given a harsher punishment than you deserved. Write about it.

From *Birthday a Day*, published by GoodYearBooks. Copyright © 1996 Stephen Currie.

Luis Muñoz Rivera

1859, Puerto Rico

How would you like to become president for your birthday? Luis did. For years Puerto Rico had been ruled by Spain. Then the island won its independence. On Luis's thirty-ninth birthday, he became the leader of the new country of Puerto Rico. It didn't last long. Nine days later, the U.S. took over. Luis was disappointed, but he worked with the U.S. government too. He wrote poems, ran a newspaper, and gave speeches to encourage Puerto Ricans to take pride in their island. Today, even Puerto Ricans who don't want independence remember Luis as a national hero.

Invent your own island. Draw a map of it.

July
18

S. I. Hayakawa
1906, British Columbia

S. I. was a professor, a cabdriver, and a U.S. Senator. But the most complicated job he ever had was being college president.

In 1968, many students believed their schools and the world were unjust. At S. I.'s college, some students protested by not going to class. They tried to keep other students from going, too, but S. I. was determined not to let that happen. Once a few students drove across campus, shouting into loudspeakers. S. I. climbed on their truck and ripped out all the microphone wires. S. I. got fifty pounds of mail about that incident!

Write a letter to S. I. supporting or complaining about what he did.

From *Birthday a Day*, published by GoodYearBooks. Copyright © 1996 Stephen Currie.

July

19

Lizzie Borden
1860, Massachusetts

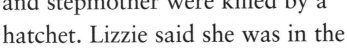

If you've heard of Lizzie, it's because of her parents. Lizzie's father and stepmother were killed by a hatchet. Lizzie said she was in the barn when the murders were committed. But the barn floor was covered with thick dust. A few days later, Lizzie burned a dress of hers that might have had bloodstains. Children chanted: "Lizzie Borden took an ax, and gave her mother forty whacks." But the jury had other ideas. No blood was found on Lizzie. No one had seen the murders committed. So the jury found Lizzie "not guilty."

Make up your own rhyme about something in the news.

July

20

Maria Van Rensselaer

1645, New York

Imagine moving from one country to another, over and over again. Now imagine that you stay in one place, but the country keeps changing. That was how things were for Maria.

Maria was a "patroon"—a wealthy landowner. Her property started off in the Dutch colony of New Amsterdam. Then the English conquered it. Next, the Dutch took it back. Finally it became English again, under the name of New York. Maria was kept busy trying to manage her land and keep it her own. After all, the laws kept changing too! In the end the colony stayed English, and the property was hers.

Make up a skit about Maria's life.

From *Birthday a Day*, published by GoodYearBooks. Copyright © 1996 Stephen Currie.

July

21

Janet Reno
1938, Florida

Janet once wanted to be the first woman baseball player. Instead, she became the first woman to be U.S. Attorney General. It wasn't as glamorous, but it was more powerful. As Attorney General, Janet was the main lawyer for the U.S. government. She helped children and figured out what to do with criminals. Many people admired Janet for her honesty and hard work. There was even a rap song written about her! But Janet enjoyed a simple life: walking to work, canoeing for fun, and taking care of her thirty-five pet peacocks—all of whom were named Horace.

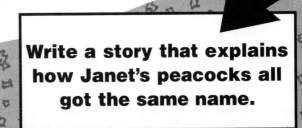

Write a story that explains how Janet's peacocks all got the same name.

July
22

William Spooner
1844, England

Keep your icicle properly boiled.

Excuse me: that should read "Keep your bicycle properly oiled." It's Filliam's wault—er, William's fault. William was a minister and a teacher, but he is remembered for mixing up the first letters of the words he said. When he tried to say "The Lord is a *l*oving *sh*epherd," it came out "a *sh*oving *l*eopard"—better be careful! Do you have a "half-*w*armed *f*ish" inside you—or rather, a "half-*f*ormed *w*ish?" In church, William was forever sewing people to their sheets. In his honor, we call this kind of mixing up a "choonerism"—beg your pardon, a "spoonerism."

Make up a spoonerism. See if you can get it to make sense.

From *Birthday a Day*, published by GoodYearBooks. Copyright © 1996 Stephen Currie.

Harriet Strong

1844, New York

Like walnuts? Talk to Harriet. She owned the largest walnut orchard in the world. Unfortunately, walnuts need a steady supply of water, and Harriet's trees were in a place that either had floods or no rain at all. So Harriet designed a system of storage dams. The dams were built into a hillside. Each pool of water helped support the dam behind it and farther up. The invention was a success, and the walnuts grew until she was called the "Walnut Queen." Harriet continued to study dams. She even proposed damming up the Grand Canyon to provide water for Los Angeles!

Use clay and water to build a dam.

Simón Bolívar

1783, Venezuela

As a young man, Simón traveled to Europe. He wasn't interested in seeing the sights, though. Instead, he was on a mission to free South America from Spanish rule. Simón talked to all the great writers and thinkers he could find. In 1810 he returned to Venezuela and started a revolution. It wasn't easy. The fight lasted more than ten years, but in the end Simón was victorious. To the people of South America, Simón was worth his weight in gold. The country of Bolivia—you can guess how it got its name!—awarded him a gold medal. Even today, Venezuelan money is called bolivars.

Draw a map of some imaginary countries. Name them after your friends.

From *Birthday a Day*, published by GoodYearBooks. Copyright © 1996 Stephen Currie.

25

Samuel Maverick
1803, *South Carolina*

Samuel was a soldier, a politician, and an explorer. But he became famous for his cattle. In the 1840s, cattle often roamed free in Texas. To tell whose was whose, each calf was branded with a special mark. Except Samuel's, that is. His neighbors knew that most unbranded calves were "Maverick's"—and the name stuck. Soon any unbranded calf was a maverick. Years later, *maverick* came to mean people who do things their own way. That fit Samuel too. Once he wounded another man in a duel. Then he carried the victim to his own house and nursed him back to health!

Think of a maverick you know. Explain what makes that person one.

George Catlin
1796, Pennsylvania

Some people save their money for summer vacation. George saved his for summers, too, but not for vacations.

George was a lawyer and a painter. Though his portraits became quite well-known, he wasn't excited about his work. Then he met some Plains Indians. Realizing that their way of life might soon be gone, George decided to spend his time painting them. He'd paint portraits at home all winter, earning money so he could afford to stay with Native Americans in the summer. In ten years he painted six hundred portraits of Native Americans, along with their games, ceremonies, and villages.

Paint or photograph your friends playing a game.

From *Birthday a Day*, published by GoodYearBooks. Copyright © 1996 Stephen Currie.

Mary Peck Butterworth

1686, Massachusetts

In colonial America, paper money was easy to counterfeit. Most methods of copying the money involved complicated printing presses, but Mary invented a simple way to do it.

First, she heated cloth and stuck a real bill to it. The hot cloth picked up the design on the bill. Then she pressed the cloth to blank paper. The design went onto the paper to make new "money." Next, Mary inked in the faintest lines with special pens made by one of her brothers. And if the police came by, it was easy to destroy the evidence. How? All she had to do was burn the cloth.

Draw a comic strip with Mary as the main character.

July

28

Beatrix Potter
1866, England

Beatrix owned a rabbit named Benjamin Bounce. Every morning Beatrix put a leash on Benjamin and took him for a walk. She tried to paint pictures of him, but he had a tendency to eat the paint. Still, Benjamin became famous. He was the model for two book characters: Benjamin Bunny and his cousin Peter Rabbit. Beatrix also kept a snail named Bill, a mouse named Xarifa, some lizards, and a few bats. They found their way into her stories too. Before publishing any books, Beatrix kept a private diary. How private was it? She wrote every entry in code!

Make up a code and write a secret message.

From *Birthday a Day*, published by GoodYearBooks. Copyright © 1996 Stephen Currie.

Sigmund Romberg

1887, Hungary

For playing piano at a restaurant, Sigmund got fifteen dollars a week, plus all the stew he could eat. Then another restaurant hired him. His new salary was twenty-five dollars and all the chicken he could eat. Next, he was making forty-five dollars at yet another restaurant. We don't know what they were feeding him!

Sigmund became famous for writing operettas—plays with music—with names like *The Student Prince* and *The New Moon*. Many of Sigmund's ideas, though, wound up in the trash. "One has to shake off failure," he said, "like a dog shakes off water." Sigmund shook well. He wrote over seventy shows.

From *Birthday a Day*, published by GoodYearBooks. Copyright © 1996 Stephen Currie.

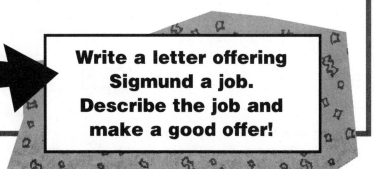

Write a letter offering Sigmund a job. Describe the job and make a good offer!

July

30

Henry Ford
1863, Michigan

Henry loved watches. He used to make money fixing his neighbors' clocks. At age twelve, he even built a watch by himself. Henry had a plan for making watches in a factory. Instead of one person building the whole watch, lots of workers would build different parts. Henry was sure this "assembly line" would be faster.

Then Henry got interested in cars. The first car he built had no reverse gear. He had to cut a hole in his workshop wall to get it out. Still, it was a start. Soon Henry was using his assembly line method to make millions of cars, instead!

Get some friends to make paper airplanes using an assembly line.

From *Birthday a Day*, published by GoodYearBooks. Copyright © 1996 Stephen Currie.

July 31

Whitney Young

1921, Kentucky

WE SHALL OVERCOME

How can you fight injustice? Some people have used weapons. Others have yelled, marched, and even gone to jail. But not Whitney. He was the man behind the people who marched, yelled, and went to jail. As head of the National Urban League, Whitney worked to make life easier for African Americans. While others yelled, Whitney talked politely to the president. While others marched, Whitney used statistics to prove his case. And while others went to jail, Whitney suggested new ideas. Which way worked? Well, both ways did. And both ways worked together.

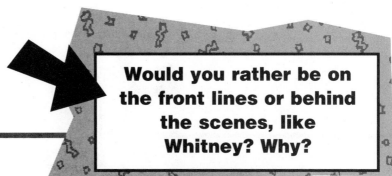

Would you rather be on the front lines or behind the scenes, like Whitney? Why?

Maria Mitchell
1818, Massachusetts

Most people who use banks go during the day. Maria visited hers only at night, and she always climbed up to the roof. Not to rob it, though. The bank's roof was the best place in town to watch the stars.

Maria ran her town's library for twenty years. When things weren't too busy, Maria read everything in sight, especially books on math and astronomy. Soon she was making careful observations of the sky. In 1847, she discovered a new comet. As Maria's work grew more famous, she became a professor of astronomy. The best part of her new job was trading in the bank roof for a real observatory!

Design a constellation of your own. Give it a name.

From *Birthday a Day*, published by GoodYearBooks. Copyright © 1996 Stephen Currie.

August

2

Pierre L'Enfant
1754, France

Pierre's last name meant "The Child," not "The Elephant." Like most small children (and most elephants), he didn't understand money. People kept hiring him to design buildings and cities. They'd tell him how much money to spend. Pierre would agree. Then he'd go out and spend three times as much. He was fired halfway through most projects. Pierre is best remembered for designing Washington, D.C. His ideas were wonderful, but the cost got him fired there too.

Years later he asked Congress to pay him for the work he'd done. He wanted $95,000. They gave him $3,800.

Design a plan for a city.

Elisha Graves Otis

1811, Vermont

Before 1852, no one used elevators very often. They were too dangerous. If the chain that supported an elevator broke, the whole thing would crash to the floor. That year, though, Elisha invented a special safety device to keep the elevator from falling. At first, no one was interested. Then Elisha demonstrated his invention in public. Standing in an elevator, he ordered the chain cut.

When it stayed in place, business owners flocked to buy an Otis elevator. Elisha never saw the Sears Tower or the Empire State Building. But without him, no skyscraper could possibly exist.

Name all the ways you can of getting from one place to another.

From *Birthday a Day*, published by GoodYearBooks. Copyright © 1996 Stephen Currie.

Raoul Wallenberg

1912, Sweden

In 1944, Raoul was sent to Hungary on a very important mission: to protect Jews from the Nazis. Raoul had plenty of money to work with, but he didn't have much time. He paid guards to let Jews leave the country. He stood in front of Jewish households, blocking the doors so soldiers couldn't take the owners away. He even printed up Swedish passports and gave them to Hungarian Jews. The Jews were not Swedish, of course, but the passports gave them official protection from the Swedish government. By the time the war ended a year later, Raoul had saved many thousands of lives.

Write down another way Raoul might have used to save Jews.

Neil Armstrong

1930, Ohio

It was one small step for a man, but one giant leap for mankind. The step was Neil's, and the place was the moon.

Growing up, Neil liked music and was active in the Boy Scouts, but his first love was airplanes. As a pilot who tested jets, Neil sometimes flew four thousand miles an hour! That experience got Neil onto the first manned moon flight. Wearing a 185-pound spacesuit, Neil spent twenty-one hours on the moon. Once on earth again, Neil spent eighteen days in isolation, just in case he carried any extraterrestrial germs. It was a small price to pay for being the first human on the moon.

Write down your experiences as the first person on Mars.

From *Birthday a Day*, published by GoodYearBooks. Copyright © 1996 Stephen Currie.

Alexander Fleming
1881, Scotland

While working in a lab, Alexander accidentally left a plate of bacteria next to a window. A few days later, it was all moldy. Instead of throwing the plate away, Alexander studied it. The mold had destroyed all the bacteria it touched. Alexander had discovered penicillin, the first medicine that could fight and kill germs. "It will save lives by thousands," Alexander predicted, and it did. Even in his spare time, Alexander liked germs. Painting was one of his hobbies. But instead of regular paint, Alexander used brightly-colored bacteria!

Try making a "painting" with mustard and ketchup.

7

Ralph Bunche
1904, Michigan

Ralph was a man full of hate and prejudice. What did he hate? Hate and prejudice.

Everywhere Ralph looked, people were having trouble getting along. Too often, disagreements between countries ended up in hatred and war. Ralph knew there must be a better way, so he went to work as a peacemaker for the United Nations. Often the countries at war were so angry, it was all Ralph could do to get them to sit down and talk. But more often than not, Ralph succeeded. He helped show the world that there are other answers besides violence.

Write about a time when you were a peacemaker.

From *Birthday a Day*, published by GoodYearBooks. Copyright © 1996 Stephen Currie.

From *Birthday a Day*, published by GoodYearBooks. Copyright © 1996 Stephen Currie.

August

8

Esther Williams
1923, California

Eight-year-old Esther loved to swim. But the beach was too far, and the pool across the street cost money. So Esther worked out a deal with the pool management. For every hundred towels she folded, she got a free hour of swimming. A good thing too! Esther became a swim champion and swimsuit model. Before long, she had a movie contract. Though Esther's movies were not very good, they were enormously popular. "I can't act," Esther admitted, but she sure could swim, and almost every movie she made had at least one water ballet sequence.

What muscles do you need most when you swim? Explain why.

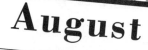

P. L. Travers

1906, Australia

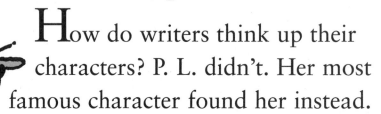

How do writers think up their characters? P. L. didn't. Her most famous character found her instead.

P. L. was recovering from an illness. Bored with everything, she thought up a story. The characters and plot came to her with such speed that she could barely keep up. When she had written it down, she showed it to a friend, who urged her to publish it. That story led to several books. It also became a play, a movie, and a piece of music. And two kinds of roses were named for the main character—a nanny called Mary Poppins.

Find a quiet place to think. Does a story character come to you?

From *Birthday a Day*, published by GoodYearBooks. Copyright © 1996 Stephen Currie.

Horace Fletcher
1849, Massachusetts

27...28...29...30......

Horace had a wonderful life. He sailed the globe hunting whales, he wrote about art, he managed an opera house, and he owned an ink factory. But then he discovered that he couldn't get life insurance because he was overweight. Horace knew why: he wasn't chewing his food properly. So he drew up "Fletcherisms," Horace's own rules for eating. The most important? Be sure to chew each mouthful thirty-two times, once for each tooth. One person said that Fletcherism "nearly killed me," but Horace's experience was different. To celebrate his fiftieth birthday, he hopped on a bike and rode two hundred miles!

Guess how long lunch will take if you chew each bite 32 times.

Carrie Jacobs Bond

1862, Wisconsin

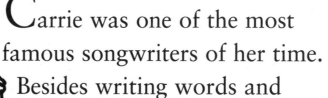

Carrie was one of the most famous songwriters of her time. Besides writing words and composing music, she sang her songs in concerts and drew pictures for the covers of the sheet music. Carrie had an early start. By age nine, she could play piano pieces after hearing them only once. Carrie wrote two songs that were especially popular. One was called "I Love You Truly." As for the other, she wrote the words after watching a sunset, and she composed the music during a moonlight drive. Sounds like a perfect day, doesn't it? Well, that's what Carrie called the song: "A Perfect Day."

Draw a picture for the cover of your favorite song.

From *Birthday a Day*, published by GoodYearBooks. Copyright © 1996 Stephen Currie.

August

12

Diamond Jim Brady
1856, New York

Jim was a banker, but he was best known for his stomach. His snacks were bigger than most people's dinners. Lunch was enough oysters, steak, and lobster for a dozen people, followed by a couple of pies or two pounds of candy. As for dinner, the chef at Jim's favorite restaurant called him "my twenty-five best customers." Jim would do anything to get the food he wanted. Once he hired a spy to get a secret recipe from a restaurant in France. Another time, Jim spent forty thousand dollars on food for a party. The guest of honor? Jim's horse.

Plan a meal for Jim or twenty-five of his friends.

August

13

Annie Oakley
1860, Ohio

LITTLE SURE SHOT

Annie had a terrible childhood. When she was very young, she worked as a servant. She was beaten and overworked. She even ran away once. But she also learned to shoot a gun. After her father died, Annie became the family hunter. Soon she was making trick shots for money. Throw a ball in the air, and Annie could hit it. Stand her on a running horse, and she could still shoot the flame off a candle. Flip a card near her and watch it come down, riddled with bullet holes. They called Annie "Little Sure Shot," and no one handled a gun better than she did.

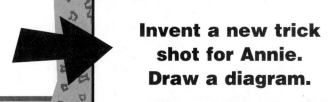

Invent a new trick shot for Annie. Draw a diagram.

From *Birthday a Day*, published by GoodYearBooks. Copyright © 1996 Stephen Currie.

Gary Larson

1950, Washington

Every time Gary went down to the basement when he was a boy, his older brother would lock the door, turn out the lights, and chant "It's coming for you, Gary!" Years later, for his comic strip *The Far Side*, Gary designed a "Monster Snorkel" which let children breathe while hiding from monsters. Any guesses where he got the idea?

Gary's cartoons were full of monsters, along with scientists, ducks, and talking insects. People either loved or hated his bizarre sense of humor. One scientist certainly appreciated it, though. He named an insect after Gary: "Strigiphilus Garylarsoni"—the biting louse.

Draw a cartoon that Gary would appreciate.

Napoleon Bonaparte

1769, France

It was nice being related to Napoleon, the emperor of France. After Napoleon conquered most of Europe, he let family members rule the countries he'd taken over. The new king of Holland was Napoleon's brother Louis; brother Joseph became king of Spain. A sister was queen in Italy, and another brother ruled part of Germany. Unfortunately for the family, it didn't last long. Napoleon lost his own power and was forced to leave France. He ended his life on an island called St. Helena, where the former emperor took three baths a day and stayed in shape by riding seesaws with the local children.

Write a short skit about Napoleon and his relatives.

From *Birthday a Day*, published by GoodYearBooks. Copyright © 1996 Stephen Currie.

Yamaga Soko
1622, Japan

When you hear the word "samurai," you probably think of a warrior with a sword. But there's a lot more to it than that. Yamaga was an expert on military tactics. He thought that fighters could be important during peacetime too. He came up with a set of rules, called "Bushido," for the samurai. Just as important as fighting, Yamaga said, samurai needed to be generous and responsible, and set a good example for everyone else. Samurai who could not follow Bushido had no business being samurai. You might guess that some samurai disagreed. You'd be right, but Yamaga's ideas won out in the end.

From *Birthday a Day*, published by GoodYearBooks.

Make a list of rules you think samurai ought to follow.

August

17

Marcus Garvey
1887, Jamaica

Today, there are about fifty different African countries. But if Marcus had had his way, there would be just one—with him in charge.

Marcus knew that many black people across the world needed money, power, and pride. To help with money, Marcus started organizations and jobs for blacks: "Black Cross" nurses, "Black Star" ships. To give blacks power, Marcus proposed a new African nation just for blacks. As for pride, Marcus spoke and wrote about black history. Not all of his ideas won favor, but black pride did.

Thanks to Marcus, many blacks became aware of their heritage for the first time.

Choose a part of the earth to be your own country. What will you call it?

From *Birthday a Day*, published by GoodYearBooks. Copyright © 1996 Stephen Currie.

Meriweather Lewis

1774, Virginia

A nearsighted explorer almost cost Meriweather his life.

When Thomas Jefferson wanted the West explored, he chose Meriweather to be one of the leaders. He thought Meriweather was brave, steady, honest, and a good scientist. In 1803, Meriweather Lewis and William Clark headed up the Missouri River. Three years later, they returned with plenty of new information: maps, charts, and scientific data. Everyone was surprised to see them. They thought all the explorers had died. In fact, Meriweather nearly had. One of his men thought he was a deer and shot him by mistake!

"Explore" part of your neighborhood. Make a map of what you see.

August
19

Orville Wright
1871, Ohio

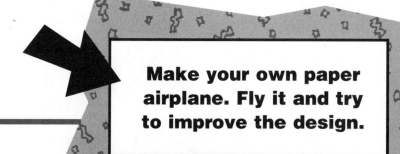

Bicycles, kites, gliders. Orville and his brother Wilbur could think of nothing but machinery and how to build an engine-powered "aeroplane." Their father thought they were crazy. The brothers took trips to places where the wind would be perfect for flying. They ran experiments in wind tunnels and built their own motors. Their first plane had no wheels, so it was launched with a catapult. Orville piloted the first flight. He lay in the cockpit; there wasn't room to sit. The flight lasted just twelve seconds, but it changed the world. We can guess that even their father was pleased.

Make your own paper airplane. Fly it and try to improve the design.

From *Birthday a Day*, published by GoodYearBooks. Copyright © 1996 Stephen Currie.

20

Connie Chung
1946, District of Columbia

Work till midnight; sleep till three in the morning. Work till noon; grab three more hours of sleep, and get ready to work again. Being a news broadcaster was a miserable life, and Connie loved every minute of it.

Connie had always liked being on stage. As a high school student, she acted in plays. Having an audience was a good experience for her career as a television reporter. Sometimes Connie announced the news. Other times, she interviewed people herself. During one presidential election, Connie arrived at a candidate's house at five o'clock every morning, just to be sure she didn't miss anything!

Announce your own news into a tape recorder.

21

Count Basie
1906, New Jersey

Count Basie wasn't actually a count; his real name was Bill. Night after night, he played jazz music for people who liked to dance, and people who just liked to listen. The Count performed on the piano and led a band. The rhythms the Count used gave his music a "jumping" quality that made audiences want to tap their toes. In North Carolina, 26,000 people showed up for one of his concerts. When most of them couldn't get into the theater, they got angry. It looked like there might even be a riot. But the Count agreed to stay and play another show, and they quieted down.

Name three qualities a musician needs. Explain why.

From *Birthday a Day*, published by GoodYearBooks. Copyright © 1996 Stephen Currie.

Dorothy Parker
1893, New Jersey

Dorothy and some other writers used to get together for lunch. They all liked to make up witty insults. Dorothy's were the cleverest—and meanest. She had a way of insulting people so they didn't even notice at first. It's a compliment to say that an actress can express all the emotions "from A to Z." In a play review, though, Dorothy changed the line to read "from A to B." When a snooty rich man died, Dorothy wrote that he could now entertain "the most exclusive worms." Once she called a book better than counting sheep. That was because—yawn—it was so boring that—zzzzz.

Read a book or watch a movie. Write a review that Dorothy would appreciate.

August

23

Oliver Perry

1785, Rhode Island

> WE HAVE MET THE ENEMY AND THEY ARE OURS.

Though Oliver was an officer in the U.S. Navy, his most famous battle was fought hundreds of miles from the nearest ocean.

Oliver joined the Navy at age fourteen. He spent the next few years sailing on the Atlantic Ocean and the Mediterranean Sea. Then the U.S. fought the War of 1812. Oliver commanded ten American ships on Lake Erie. His job was to win control of the lake from Great Britain. The battle was fierce. Oliver's best ship was damaged, but he held on and won. To announce the victory, he sent a famous message. "We have met the enemy," it read, "and they are ours."

Make a list of all the kinds of boats you can think of.

From *Birthday a Day*, published by GoodYearBooks. Copyright © 1996 Stephen Currie.

Angie Brooks

1928, Liberia

At age eleven, Angie earned money typing legal papers. She disliked some of the laws she was typing up, so she decided to be a lawyer. Because she didn't have money for law school, she went to the president of Liberia to ask for help. When he wouldn't see her in his office, she followed him during his morning walk so she could talk to him. It worked. Angie became the first woman lawyer in Liberia. Later, she served as president of the United Nations. Angie worked especially hard to help kids. She had as many as nineteen foster children every year!

Act out the discussion between Angie and the Liberian president.

Allan Pinkerton
1819, Scotland

WE NEVER SLEEP

Allan made wooden barrels. One day, while cutting wood, he stumbled on a gang of counterfeiters. After helping the police capture the criminals, Allan quit making barrels. Catching crooks was much more interesting! Instead, he opened his own private detective agency. It did well; Allan was organized and he worked hard. In 1861, he stopped a plot to assassinate Abraham Lincoln. A few years later, he solved a famous robbery in which $700,000 had been stolen. His symbol was an open eye above the words "We Never Sleep."

Design your own symbol for a detective agency.

August

26

Joseph Montgolfier
1740, France

The first airline passengers were a duck, a sheep, and a rooster. They got to fly for free. Of course, the trip lasted just eight minutes, and the airline wasn't much. It was only a basket under a bag full of smoke—a giant hot-air balloon.

The balloon was the work of Joseph and his brother Jacques. One day Joseph saw his wife's dress drying by a fire. As the hot smoke rose, the dress billowed out, and Joseph got the idea for the balloon. For the first flight, they sewed an enormous cloth bag and filled it with smoke from a fire. How did the animals like the trip? Sorry. They never said—never even sent a postcard!

Make a parachute with cloth, paper, and string.

From *Birthday a Day*, published by GoodYearBooks. Copyright © 1996 Stephen Currie.

Mother Teresa
1910, Macedonia

What would you do if your school principal gave you a limousine? Well, that's not what Mother Teresa did. When the Roman Catholic Pope gave one to her, she didn't use it once. She auctioned it off and used the money to build a hospital. That was normal for Mother Teresa. Every gift went to help people in need. A nun from the time she was eighteen, she devoted her life to serving the people she called "the poorest of the poor." To do that properly, Mother Teresa felt she needed to be poor herself. It made sense. Still, it would be hard to resist just one little ride in that limo. . . .

Which three things that you own would be hardest to give up?

From *Birthday a Day*, published by GoodYearBooks. Copyright © 1996 Stephen Currie.

28

Roger Tory Peterson
1908, New York

Roger hated school. He did badly, and his behavior was a problem. Then Roger joined a nature club and found that he liked birds. Most of all, he liked identifying birds by studying their shape, size, color, and special markings. The more he watched, the better his schoolwork became.

Roger became an art teacher, but he still watched birds. In 1934, Roger combined his two interests. He wrote a "field guide" to birds, a book which told how to identify them, and painted the pictures himself. His methods were so good, the army used them to teach soldiers how to tell airplanes apart!

Go on a bird walk. How many birds can you identify?

Abby Hutchinson

1829, New Hampshire

America has always had plenty of family singing groups. But there weren't any quite like Abby and her family. To begin with, there were more Hutchinsons than Trapps, Osmonds, Jacksons, or anybody else: thirteen singers in all. Often all thirteen sang together. When it was just Abby and a few of the boys, people called them "a nest of brothers with a sister in it."

Besides being good musicians, Abby and her family had strong opinions. They supported women's rights and hated slavery. Before the Civil War, they actually paid runaway slaves to come to their concerts!

Draw your family as a singing group. What kind of music would you and your family sing?

From *Birthday a Day*, published by GoodYearBooks. Copyright © 1996 Stephen Currie.

30

Mary Shelley

1797, England

One evening, Mary and three friends sat around the fire, telling ghost stories. Someone suggested they should make up spooky stories themselves and write them down. A few days later, Mary dreamed of a hideous corpse coming to life. "What terrified me," she said to herself, "will terrify others." She wrote the scene just as she'd dreamed it. That became the basis of *Frankenstein,* which was published the next year. Who was Frankenstein? Not who you think. In Mary's book, Frankenstein wasn't the monster, but the scientist who brought him to life.

Write a story about a monster.

Edwin Moses

1955, Ohio

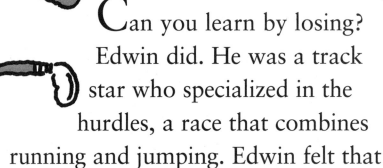

Can you learn by losing? Edwin did. He was a track star who specialized in the hurdles, a race that combines running and jumping. Edwin felt that losing could be positive. Of course, Edwin didn't have many learning experiences like that. For eleven years he never lost—he had 107 wins in a row! As a boy, though, Edwin preferred books and science projects to running. He got a college scholarship because of his grades, not his speed. In 1984, Edwin was given the honor of taking the Olympic oath. He promised that all the athletes would work hard and be good sports. Then he went out and won another race.

Set up your own hurdle course. Try running it. Time yourself.

September

1

Seiji Ozawa
1935, Japan

When orchestra conductors wave their arms, they are actually giving signals to the musicians. One signal keeps the beat going; others tell the orchestra when to start and how loudly to play. Seiji became a great conductor—literally by accident.

As a boy, Seiji studied piano. During a soccer game, though, he fell and broke two fingers. For nearly a year he couldn't play the piano at all. To pass the time, Seiji took up conducting. He loved it. When his fingers were healed, Seiji's piano career was over. But his long and successful career as a conductor was just beginning.

Get some friends together. Conduct them in a song.

Liliuokalani
1838, Hawaii

Many American songs are about certain states. There's "My Old Kentucky Home" and "Sweet Home Alabama." Then there's Liliuokalani's song "Aloha Oe," which is about Hawaii. It's the most famous American song written by a queen!

Liliuokalani was queen of Hawaii. She was the last queen to rule any part of the United States. As ruler, she set up schools for Hawaiian children. When Hawaii became part of the U.S., Liliuokalani lost her power. But she wasn't forgotten. Important visitors to Hawaii didn't just stop by to see the new governor. They came to visit the old queen, as well.

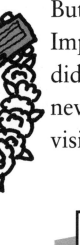

Draw what you think Liliuokalani might have worn as queen.

3

Prudence Crandall

1803, Rhode Island

Prudence ran a school in Connecticut. She was well respected. Then an African American family enrolled their daughter. When whites took their children out in protest, Prudence filled their places with other African American girls. The neighbors were horrified. They polluted the well and broke the windows. They put Prudence in jail for a night. In the end, they burned down the school. Prudence had made plenty of enemies. Still, outside the town she won friends. Many Americans were upset that a person could be jailed just for trying to teach. Though Prudence was one of the first to start a school for African American children, she was not to be the last.

> **Write an on-the-scene news report about something the neighbors did to Prudence's school.**

From *Birthday a Day*, published by GoodYearBooks. Copyright © 1996 Stephen Currie.

September 4

Daniel Burnham
1846, New York

In German, it's a "Wolkenkratzer"—cloud-scratcher. In French, it's a "gratte-ciel"—sky-grater. And in English, it's called a—

Daniel designed one of the first skyscrapers. Though it was only ten stories tall, it started a trend. But then, Daniel started quite a few trends. Every time he planned a city, he built wide streets. Soon almost all city planners were designing wide streets. Whenever he could, Daniel put parks near his buildings. In a few years, so did everyone else. When Daniel died on a trip to Europe, all the other builders went—well, not exactly. Nobody wanted to follow a trend like that!

Design a skyscraper. Build it with dominoes or Legos®.

From *Birthday a Day*, published by GoodYearBooks. Copyright © 1996 Stephen Currie.

5

Jesse James
1857, Missouri

Can a bowl of chili protect a bank? According to one story about Jesse, it did. Jesse was an outlaw who robbed trains and banks. But he stayed away from the bank in McKinney, Texas. Why? Jesse's favorite chili restaurant was in McKinney, and he wanted to be able to eat there without being arrested.

Some people hated Jesse. Others called him a "friend to the poor." A story said he once paid a poor woman's rent, and then stole his money back from the landlord. Maybe the landlord should have offered Jesse chili instead!

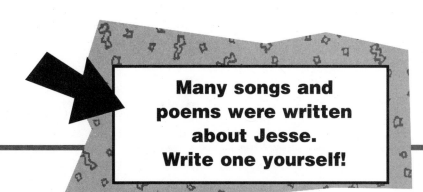

Many songs and poems were written about Jesse. Write one yourself!

From *Birthday a Day*, published by GoodYearBooks. Copyright © 1996 Stephen Currie.

September

6

Jane Addams
1860, Illinois

Though Jane had plenty of money, she chose to live in the poorest section of Chicago. There she ran a community center. She built playgrounds and gyms for children who had once played in the streets. Jane ran day-care centers and cooking classes for parents. Two thousand people a week used the center, which Jane called "Hull House." Jane was used to doing things herself. When the trash in her neighborhood didn't get picked up, she got herself appointed garbage inspector. Every morning at six she followed the trash collectors on their rounds. It drove them crazy. But it got the garbage picked up on time!

Draw what you think would be needed in a community center.

From *Birthday a Day*, published by GoodYearBooks. Copyright © 1996 Stephen Currie.

Grandma Moses

1860, New York

As a child, Anna Mary Moses used grape juice to paint pictures. As a grandmother, she took up painting again. This time she used real paint. Anna Mary painted scenes of her childhood on a farm. She gave her pictures titles like *Sugaring Off* and *Apple Pickers*. Before long, an art dealer saw her work. He bought everything she'd painted and asked for more. Anna Mary obliged, painting two thousand pictures in all. To save paint and time, she worked on several pictures at once. First she painted all the skies, then all the hills, and so forth. At age one hundred, she was still going strong!

Paint three pictures using Anna Mary's method.

From *Birthday a Day*, published by GoodYearBooks. Copyright © 1996 Stephen Currie.

Richard the Lionhearted

1157, England

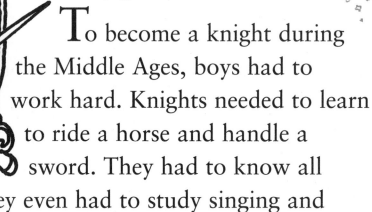

To become a knight during the Middle Ages, boys had to work hard. Knights needed to learn to ride a horse and handle a sword. They had to know all about armor. They even had to study singing and good manners.

Richard was a knight with the courage of a lion. He was king of England, too, but it was hard to tell. He didn't spend much time there. He was too busy being a knight. First he traveled to the Middle East to fight. On the way back he was captured and sent to prison in Italy. When he was released, did he go home to rule? Nope. Instead, he went out and attacked France.

Cut cardboard into the shape of a shield. Draw a design on it.

From *Birthday a Day*, published by GoodYearBooks. Copyright © 1996 Stephen Currie.

September 9

Colonel Harland Sanders

1890, Indiana

Name a job. "Colonel" Harland Sanders probably had it: ferryboat pilot, train conductor, farmer, soldier, salesperson, and many more. Then Harland opened a gas station on a Kentucky highway. Travelers often stopped during Harland's family's dinner hour, so Harland cooked extra to feed them too. They especially liked his fried chicken. Harland had made up his own recipe, using eleven secret spices. The chicken was so popular, Harland opened his own restaurant and called it Kentucky Fried Chicken. In his office, Harland kept a cage containing a pet. A chicken? Sorry—a gerbil.

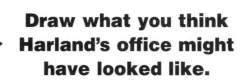

Draw what you think Harland's office might have looked like.

September 10

Fay Wray
1907, Alberta

Fay appeared in over one hundred movies. In her most famous part, her co-star was made of rubber and was less than two feet tall. Not E. T.—King Kong. Most of the shots of King Kong were really of a model. Fay played the woman that King Kong kept trying to capture. For scenes of Fay being grabbed, the technical crew built an eight-foot long furry arm that worked like a crane. King Kong's "fingers" were attached around Fay's waist. Then she was raised ten feet in the air, kicking and screaming. In fact, Fay got the role partly because she could scream so well!

Make a clay model of a movie monster.

From *Birthday a Day*, published by GoodYearBooks. Copyright © 1996 Stephen Currie.

September 11

O. Henry

1862, North Carolina

OH, HENRY

William Sydney Porter wrote stories: hundreds and hundreds of stories. In 1909 alone, he wrote sixty-five stories and published them all. Not everybody knew he was a writer, though, because William signed his work "O. Henry." Why O. Henry? One tale says William owned a cat named Henry the Proud, which would only answer to "Oh, Henry!"

William's stories could be funny, exciting, or sad. He based many of his characters on the people he met. William had just two rules for writing. Rule 1: Write stories that please yourself. Rule 2: There is no Rule 2.

Write a story. Follow William's rules.

From *Birthday a Day*, published by GoodYearBooks. Copyright © 1996 Stephen Currie.

Marie Ahnighito Peary

1893, Greenland

Marie's father, Robert, explored the Arctic. Marie's mother sometimes joined him. Marie was born during an expedition. The Eskimos nearby were fascinated by her pale skin and called her "Snowbaby." The name stuck! Marie spent her first winter in the darkness of the far North. When spring came, she was dazzled by sunbeams and tried to pick them up off the floor. The Pearys soon returned to the U.S., where Marie found that being an explorer's daughter was difficult. Once she begged her father to stop exploring. "I don't want people to think me an orphan," she said. But Robert went anyway.

Draw the sunbeams the way Marie might have seen them.

From *Birthday a Day*, published by GoodYearBooks. Copyright © 1996 Stephen Currie.

Milton Hershey
1857, Pennsylvania

Nine-year-old Milton didn't like working for a printer, so he dropped his hat into the printing press and got himself fired. For a while he earned money by selling caramels. Then he heard of a new invention called "milk chocolate." It was rich and sweet, not like the bitter, grainy chocolate that most Americans ate. It was cheap to make too. Milton started a candy factory and sold milk chocolate bars for low prices. Soon, the boy who hated printing was using more silver ink than any printer on earth. Why? To print HERSHEY'S® on the wrappers of the candy that made him famous!

Make up a recipe for a great candy bar that no one has invented yet. Give it an unusual name.

September

14

Ivan Pavlov
1849, Russia

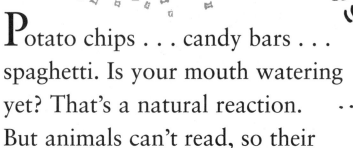

Potato chips . . . candy bars . . . spaghetti. Is your mouth watering yet? That's a natural reaction. But animals can't read, so their mouths only water if they see or smell food—correct?

Ivan did an experiment to check. He brought some dogs into his lab. Each day, he rang a little bell just before he fed them. When the dogs saw and smelled their food, their mouths watered. After a while, Ivan rang the bell, but didn't bring in any food. The dogs' mouths watered anyway. Just as you've learned that "P-I-Z-Z-A" stands for something good, the dogs had learned that the sound of the bell meant food!

Write a short skit about Ivan and his experiment.

From *Birthday a Day*, published by GoodYearBooks. Copyright © 1996 Stephen Currie.

Jan Matzeliger

1852, Surinam

From *Birthday a Day*, published by GoodYearBooks. Copyright © 1996 Stephen Currie.

"Lasting" a shoe means attaching the bottom to the top. Once, lasting could only be done by hand. It took time and skill, and it added a lot to the cost of shoes. Then Jan got to work. He had worked with machinery since he was ten. He also studied science and painting. Experimenting late at night with wood, wire, and a cigar box, Jan invented a lasting machine. Though it was complicated, it really worked. He was offered fifty dollars for it, then fifteen hundred dollars, but Jan started his own company instead. His machine could last shoes ten times faster than before. And using it made shoes much cheaper to buy.

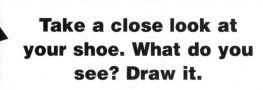

Take a close look at your shoe. What do you see? Draw it.

Nadia Boulanger

1887, France

For seventy years, Nadia shared an apartment with two pianos and an organ. She was a music teacher. Her students liked to say that she knew everything there was to know about music. She needed to, because Nadia did not always treat her students nicely. Sometimes she whacked their hands with a ruler if they played wrong notes. When her students tried to write music, she often told them that their ideas were "forbidden." Still, Nadia had her fans. For years, almost every young American who wanted to be a composer studied with her— even if it might be painful!

Draw a comic strip about Nadia and her students.

From *Birthday a Day*, published by GoodYearBooks. Copyright © 1996 Stephen Currie.

Robert Matsui
1941, California

Ｈow would you like to go to "internment camp"? You wouldn't. It was really a jail. The U.S. was fighting a war against Japan, and the government was worried that Japanese Americans might be spies. Just in case, many Americans were taken from their homes and sent to the camps. That even included people who'd been U.S. citizens for years, and babies like Robert. Robert knew little of this terrible time until he was an adult. As a member of Congress, though, Robert helped pass a bill that did two things. It gave money to camp survivors, and it apologized to them.

Write about the worst thing that ever happened to you.

18

Greta Garbo
1905, Sweden

In a 1931 movie, Greta played a character who said "I want to be alone." Greta agreed completely.

Many people thought Greta was the most beautiful woman in the world. As a teenager, she modeled hats in a department store. Soon she became a movie star. But Greta valued her privacy more than anything. She rarely answered questions about herself. Though her movies were tremendously popular, Greta quit making them when she was just thirty-six. When she retired, Greta even traveled using other people's names so she could be truly "alone."

Suppose Greta agreed to let you interview her. What would you want to know? Why?

From *Birthday a Day*, published by GoodYearBooks. Copyright © 1996 Stephen Currie.

From *Birthday a Day*, published by GoodYearBooks. Copyright © 1996 Stephen Currie.

September

19

Twiggy
1949, England

When Twiggy was only a teenager, she was already one of the world's richest models. Her picture was on magazine covers everywhere, and her name was worth millions. Companies paid to make Twiggy dolls, Twiggy makeup kits, and Twiggy lunchboxes. There were official Twiggy pens, a Twiggy game, and a TV special called *Twiggy in Movieland*. Since Twiggy was not yet an adult, all her money went to her parents, who kept it for her. Twiggy's real name was Leslie Hornby. She was called Twiggy because she was shaped like a twig—almost unbelievably skinny!

Design some toys and souvenirs named after yourself.

Red Cloud
1822, Nebraska

The choice for Sioux Indian leader came down to two men. One was Red Cloud. The other was called "Young Man Afraid of His Horses." It was an easy choice.

As chief, Red Cloud opposed whites who came into his territory. Unlike most other Native American leaders, though, Red Cloud was pretty successful. When the U.S. army built three new forts, Red Cloud attacked any soldiers who tried to get to them. After two years of this, the U.S. agreed to abandon the forts. Even then, Red Cloud insisted that the forts be burned. He never did trust the government!

Make up a story telling how Red Cloud got his name.

From *Birthday a Day*, published by GoodYearBooks. Copyright © 1996 Stephen Currie.

H. G. Wells

1866, England

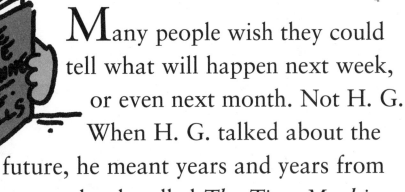

Many people wish they could tell what will happen next week, or even next month. Not H. G. When H. G. talked about the future, he meant years and years from now. Once he wrote a book called *The Time Machine*. It was set in the year 802701!

H. G. taught science and wrote books about the future. These became some of the first "science fiction" stories. His tales involved space travel and aliens visiting Earth. They also predicted what humans will look like a million years from now. H. G. never found out if his predictions came true. He lived to be seventy-nine. It wasn't nearly long enough!

Write your own tale of the future.

Mrs. Astor
1830, New York

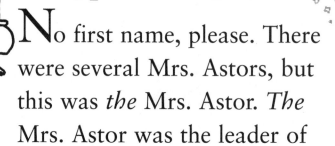

No first name, please. There were several Mrs. Astors, but this was *the* Mrs. Astor. *The* Mrs. Astor was the leader of the New York City social scene. She made a list of the four hundred most important people in town. Each year she invited them all over for a fancy ball. People who offended her were dropped from the list, so her friends did what she wanted. When Mrs. Astor left a theater, everybody who was anybody left too. Her dinner parties were incredibly boring, but no one dared to skip them. That would be as bad as calling Mrs. Astor by her real first name, Caroline, to tell her apart from all those other Mrs. Astors.

Imagine a conversation at one of Mrs. Astor's boring dinner parties. Write it down.

From *Birthday a Day*, published by GoodYearBooks. Copyright © 1996 Stephen Currie.

Mary Church Terrell

1863, Tennessee

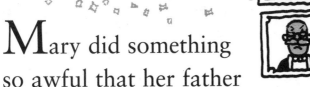

Mary did something so awful that her father cut her out of his will. Her friends warned her it would mean she could never get married. What horrible thing did Mary do? At a time when most women didn't get jobs, she—gulp—went to college to study teaching and mathematics!

Fortunately, Mary didn't pay any attention to her father and friends. She had quite a nice life. Mary served on school boards. She worked for fair pay for nurses, waitresses, and maids. At age ninety, she led a demonstration against a restaurant that wouldn't serve African Americans. She got married too. And she did it all even though she knew math!

Imagine you were Mary. Write a letter to Mary's father.

From *Birthday a Day*, published by GoodYearBooks. Copyright © 1996 Stephen Currie.

Jim Henson
1936, Mississippi

The next time you see Kermit the Frog, Miss Piggy, or any of the rest of the Muppets, be glad that Jim's mother liked to wear green.

Jim belonged to a puppet club in high school. One day he heard that a TV station was running an audition for young puppeteers. Jim didn't have any puppets worth entering, so he made one. The only material he could find was his mom's old green coat. Jim made a frog from it and won the contest. That coat was the beginning of Kermit. It's fun to imagine what would have happened if Mrs. Henson's coat had been another color. Would a red coat have become "Kermit the Fox"?

Create your own puppet using some scrap cloth.

From *Birthday a Day*, published by GoodYearBooks. Copyright © 1996 Stephen Currie.

Ch'ien Lung
1711, China

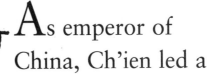

As emperor of China, Ch'ien led a well-ordered life. At six each morning he got up, bathed, and ate breakfast. Next, Ch'ien studied reports and talked to advisors. Then came lunch, a rest period, and time to read and paint. After dinner, Ch'ien saw his nineteen children or attended plays.

Ch'ien made China a very powerful country. He liked the arts too. Once he asked scholars to choose the most important Chinese writings and copy them into a book. It took 36,275 volumes! At a time when few people even lived to be fifty, Ch'ien ruled China for more than sixty years.

Describe your ideal day if you were a king. Make up a schedule.

From *Birthday a Day*, published by GoodYearBooks. Copyright © 1996 Stephen Currie.

John Chapman

1774, Massachusetts

As a boy, John used to wander off in search of flowers and birds. Even as an adult, John was interested in nature and not much else. A gentle man, he was more at home with animals than people. John was said to wear an old coffee sack for a shirt, with holes cut in for the arms and the neck. When he needed a hat, he put on a tin pot.

But John's love of nature made him famous. Wherever he walked, he scattered seeds he'd gathered from herbs and fruit trees. He gave travelers bags of seeds to take with them and plant. Those seeds gave him a nickname you'll recognize: "Johnny Appleseed."

Go on a seed hunt. Where will you look? How many can you find?

From *Birthday a Day*, published by GoodYearBooks. Copyright © 1996 Stephen Currie.

27

Harry Blackstone

1885, Illinois

During a party at the White House, Harry stole a pen belonging to the president and a wallet belonging to another guest. He even stole a gun from the president's bodyguard! But he wasn't arrested. Harry was a magician.

Harry was famous for giving away rabbits after every show—once he'd pulled them out of a hat, that is! He had several favorite tricks. He could make a handkerchief "dance" around the stage. Harry made light bulbs float and ropes stand on end. He even made camels and elephants disappear. Unfortunately, he never did figure out a way to get rid of mosquitoes.

Explain one way Harry might have made a handkerchief dance.

September
28

David Walker
1785, North Carolina

Many "abolitionists," people who opposed slavery, thought slaves should be freed over time instead of all at once. David disagreed. His father had been a slave, and David knew what it was like. David ran a clothing store and worked for an African American newspaper. In 1829, David wrote a booklet called *Walker's Appeal.* In it he urged slaves to attack their owners. David knew this booklet might spell trouble. What he didn't know was that it would cost him his life. The next year, David's body was found lying in the doorway of his shop. No one ever found out who was responsible.

Imagine you were a detective. How would you investigate David's death?

From *Birthday a Day*, published by GoodYearBooks. Copyright © 1996 Stephen Currie.

29

Lech Walesa
1943, Poland

Lech used to say that the Polish government made people "forget they are human beings." The Poles were not free to do and say what they wanted. Many workers didn't have proper food and shelter. Lech decided to do something about it. He led his fellow workers in strikes, where they went off the job until they were given better pay and more freedom. Soon Lech's organization, called Solidarity, was all over Poland. The government often threatened Lech. He was offered money to stop the strikes. But Lech didn't quit. In the end he helped bring a new and fairer government to Poland.

Make up a campaign slogan for Lech and Solidarity.

William Wrigley
1861, Pennsylvania

As a young man, William went from door to door selling soap and baking powder. Customers who bought a lot from him were given sticks of chewing gum as a prize. William soon discovered that some people were buying the soap and baking powder just to get the gum. So he went into the gum business instead. The first two flavors he produced are no longer around. They were called Vassar Gum and Wrigley's Lotta Gum. But William's third flavor, Juicy Fruit, was a big success. Just as well. It wouldn't be much fun to chew "Wrigley's Scouring Soap"!

Do a survey about people's favorite flavors of gum. Make a graph.

From *Birthday a Day*, published by GoodYearBooks. Copyright © 1996 Stephen Currie.

Julie Andrews

1935, England

It would be pretty neat to star in one of the world's most popular movies. Julie starred in two. Oddly enough, she played a babysitter in each one. In *The Sound of Music,* Julie was nanny for seven children. In *Mary Poppins,* she only took care of two. In real life, though, Julie didn't babysit much. There wasn't time. Her career began when she was young. At age twelve she was already a professional singer and actress. By twenty she was a Broadway star. In the little spare time she had, Julie liked skiing, boating, and horseback riding—not to mention eating cream cheese and jelly sandwiches!

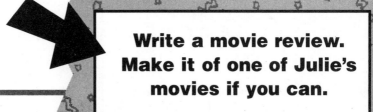

Write a movie review. Make it of one of Julie's movies if you can.

October 2

Mohandas Gandhi
1869, India

Is it ever good to be arrested?

For Mohandas Gandhi, it was. Mohandas was called "Mahatma," which means "Great Soul." He helped India get its independence from Great Britain. Mohandas kept breaking laws and going to jail for what he believed. Every time he was arrested, his followers got more determined. Not only that, the rest of the world noticed. Other nations reminded the British government that Mohandas's protests didn't hurt anyone. In fact, Mohandas didn't even believe in violence. Mohandas caused the British more trouble in jail than he did on the loose!

Make up a skit about the British arresting Mohandas.

From *Birthday a Day*, published by GoodYearBooks. Copyright © 1996 Stephen Currie.

John Ross
1790, Tennessee

John was chief of the Cherokee Indians. In many ways, John was a typical American. He served in the army. He liked the Constitution so much, he had the Cherokee write one of their own. He even owned a farm with many African slaves—just like his white neighbors. But when the U.S. decided it wanted the Cherokee lands, no one cared how American John was. Though John argued, the Cherokee were sent to Oklahoma. One out of every four Cherokee who started the trip died on the way, including John's own wife. Ever since, that awful journey has been called "The Trail of Tears."

Imagine you were on the "Trail of Tears." Draw or write about it.

4

George Sanchez
1906, New Mexico

Why speak one language when you can speak two?

George grew up speaking both English and Spanish. Even before he finished his college degree, he was teaching school. He noticed that many schools tried to make Spanish-speaking children speak English. To George, this didn't make sense. He believed that children who spoke Spanish at home would learn better if their language wasn't ignored at school. As George talked about his ideas, he found that many teachers agreed with him. If children at your school learn in different languages, say "Gracias, George!"

Learn a few words in another language. Teach them to a friend.

From *Birthday a Day*, published by GoodYearBooks. Copyright © 1996 Stephen Currie.

Maya Lin
1959, Ohio

When Maya was in college, she entered a contest. The U.S. government wanted a memorial to honor soldiers who had fought in the Vietnam War. Maya designed two long black walls, coming together in a V and listing all the soldiers killed during the war. Her plan was chosen. She predicted that the wall would be a peaceful and gentle place, and she was right. More

than a million visitors come each year to see it and find names of friends and relatives. Maya went on to design stage sets, parks, and other monuments. She also made sculptures out of metal and broken glass!

Design a memorial. What will it honor?

Fannie Lou Hamer

1917, Mississippi

Fannie used to say she was "sick and tired of being sick and tired." So she decided to do something about it. Though she was a citizen of the United States, Fannie had a hard time voting. Many whites where she lived didn't want African Americans to vote. When she tried, she was threatened and beaten. But Fannie didn't give up. She worked to make sure African Americans across the South could vote safely, without being bullied or shot. When things got tough, she'd lift her spirits with songs like "We Shall Not Be Moved" or "Oh, Freedom." And she'd remember how sick and tired she was of being sick and tired.

What are you sick and tired of? Write about it.

Desmond Tutu

1931, South Africa

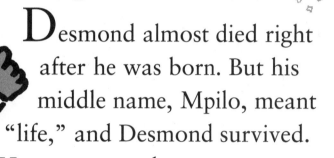

Desmond almost died right after he was born. But his middle name, Mpilo, meant "life," and Desmond survived. He went on to become a teacher, priest, and bishop. He fought for blacks' rights in a country where racism was the law. Desmond often got in trouble with the government. Once an American university wanted to give him an award. Desmond wasn't allowed to leave South Africa, so the college brought it to him instead. "Justice is going to win," Desmond always said, and he was right. In 1994, blacks came to power in South Africa. Desmond was so proud, he said he'd grown two extra inches.

Describe an event in your own life that has made you feel two inches taller.

October 8

Mary Pennington
1872, Tennessee

Next time you open the refrigerator to get a snack, think of Mary. Her work helped make sure your food won't spoil.

As a girl, Mary read a book about chemistry and decided to become a scientist. Her main interest was keeping food safe. How could you build a refrigerator so cold air couldn't escape? Mary designed one. How cool did food need to be to keep bacteria from spoiling it? Mary took temperatures and came up with answers. Even after work, Mary kept experimenting. When she invited friends over for dinner, she served them food that had been frozen in different ways!

Take some juice out of the refrigerator. How quickly does it warm up?

From *Birthday a Day*, published by GoodYearBooks. Copyright © 1996 Stephen Currie.

9

Mary Ann Shadd Cary
1823, Delaware

According to people who knew her, Mary had "bright sharp eyes that look right through you." Eyes like that made Mary an excellent teacher. She founded schools in three states, but her greatest work was done with runaway slaves in Canada. Slaves who escaped from the South were free once they'd gotten out of the U.S. But most of them were poor and couldn't read. To help out, Mary went to Canada and opened a school for the children of the runaways. Later on, she began a newspaper for them. Mary never stopped working. At age forty-six she started studying for a law degree!

Draw a map that shows how you could "escape" from your classroom.

Earle Dickson

1892, Tennessee

Earle's wife, Josephine, was pretty clumsy. She kept cutting her fingers and scraping her elbows. Covering the wounds was complicated. After cleaning the cut, Josephine had to wrap it with long, thin cloth and tie the ends. Quite a trick with one arm bleeding and no one around to help! Earle couldn't do much for his wife's clumsiness, but he figured out a way to help her, even when he wasn't home. He attached a strip of cloth to some adhesive tape. The new bandage stuck to Josephine's skin, so she could put it on easily. Sound familiar? It should. Earle had invented the "Band-Aid."

Try out three brands of plastic bandages. Which works best? Why?

From *Birthday a Day*, published by GoodYearBooks. Copyright © 1996 Stephen Currie.

Eleanor Roosevelt

1884, New York

Though Eleanor's husband, Franklin, was president, Eleanor was nearly as famous as he was. She was everywhere—visiting soldiers, talking to children, and letting her opinions be known. Eleanor wrote newspaper columns. After Franklin's death, she worked for the United Nations. For many years Eleanor was the most admired woman in the world. Her work for justice helped win her the nickname "the conscience of her generation." That wasn't Eleanor's only nickname, of course. As First Lady, she was so enthusiastic, she was called "Public Energy Number One."

What nickname would you most like to have? Why?

October

12

Perle Mesta
1889, Michigan

How many children were at the last birthday party you went to? Double it. Now double it again, and again, and maybe even again, and you have some idea how many people came to Perle's parties. The best time in Perle's life was when Harry Truman was president. Harry's wife hated to plan big parties, so Perle took over instead. She entertained royalty, actors, and politicians, and she did it well. Then she was made one of the first female ambassadors and went off to Europe—where she continued to give parties, of course!

→ **Plan a Perle-sized party. Plan food and decorations and make a shopping list.**

From *Birthday a Day*, published by GoodYearBooks. Copyright © 1996 Stephen Currie.

Molly Pitcher

1754, New Jersey

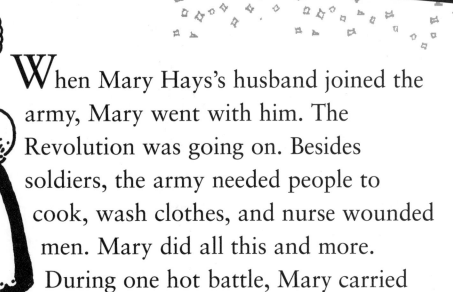

When Mary Hays's husband joined the army, Mary went with him. The Revolution was going on. Besides soldiers, the army needed people to cook, wash clothes, and nurse wounded men. Mary did all this and more. During one hot battle, Mary carried pitchers of water to the troops. Then her husband suddenly collapsed. Mary dropped her pitcher and took his place. She spent the rest of the battle firing a cannon. Years later, the state of Pennsylvania gave her a soldier's pension for her work that day. And forever afterward, Mary was known as "Molly Pitcher."

Make up a skit about Molly. Act it out.

October

14

Sheila Young
1950, Michigan

At age two, Sheila learned to ice skate. At four, she could ride a bike without training wheels. At twenty-two, Sheila was a world champion. In which sport? Both!

Sheila's first interest was speed skating. "I love the feeling of going fast," she said once. During summers she kept up her strength by cycling, which uses many of the same muscles as skating does. Soon she was so good at cycling, she began competing in both sports. Sheila said her success came partly from her parents' encouragement, partly from hard work—and partly from not wearing socks while she was skating!

Name three qualities an athlete must have. Why?

From *Birthday a Day*, published by GoodYearBooks. Copyright © 1996 Stephen Currie.

October

15

Isabella Bishop
1831, England

Isabella's husband used to say that Isabella loved traveling even more than she loved him. It was probably true!

Though Isabella liked to travel, she didn't much like fine hotels and good roads. In Malaysia, she rode an elephant. In Hawaii, she climbed a volcano, which burned the boots off her feet. Isabella ate with apes, crossed raging rivers, and once rode a horse a thousand miles. She visited India, Korea, Australia, Morocco, Canada, Egypt, China, Turkey, and many other countries. Oddly, Isabella began traveling because of poor health. Bet you'd never have guessed from her adventures!

Look at a map. Find as many of these countries as you can.

From *Birthday a Day*, published by GoodYearBooks. Copyright © 1996 Stephen Currie.

October 16

Noah Webster
1758, Connecticut

Having a conversation with Noah could be difficult. Every time you spoke to him, he'd nod his head vigorously. Then he'd take out a little notebook that he carried wherever he went, and write down some of the words you'd used. He wasn't being rude. He was just writing a dictionary, the first one published in America. Noah put in seventy thousand words, which he got from reading books and from listening to people talk. Though he expected to finish quickly, the whole project took twenty years. Noah also wrote spelling books, so if speling is hard for yew, blaim Noa—er, blame Noah.

Make up some new words. Write definitions for them.

From *Birthday a Day*, published by GoodYearBooks. Copyright © 1996 Stephen Currie.

October

17

Evel Knievel
1938, Montana

Some people call motorcycle racing dangerous. But for Evel it wasn't nearly dangerous enough. After all, he only broke two bones during races. Evel wanted more adventure. So he started riding his motorcycle through fire. Next, he jumped it over a pit filled with live rattlesnakes. He built ramps and sailed across cars, too. Soon he could jump twenty in a row. When that got boring, Evel turned his motorcycle into a miniature rocket and tried to jet over canyons. Of course, all this was a little hard on Evel's body. It was said he broke every bone except his neck at least once.

Build a ramp. How far can you send a toy car or a marble off its end?

From *Birthday a Day*, published by GoodYearBooks. Copyright © 1996 Stephen Currie.

Wynton Marsalis

1961, Louisiana

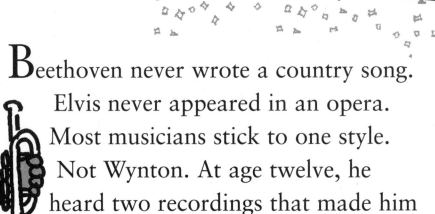

Beethoven never wrote a country song. Elvis never appeared in an opera. Most musicians stick to one style. Not Wynton. At age twelve, he heard two recordings that made him decide to become a musician. One was jazz. The other was classical. The pieces were very different, but Wynton loved each of them. For the next few years, he spent his time practicing both styles on his trumpet. People told him he'd have to choose between them. But Wynton never did. In 1984, he won an award for the best jazz performance of the year—and another for the best classical recording!

Listen to two different styles of music. Which do you like better? Why?

From *Birthday a Day*, published by GoodYearBooks. Copyright © 1996 Stephen Currie.

October

19

Amanda Theodosia Jones

1835, New York

Amanda believed in the spirit world. Once she felt in her bones that she was "wanted in Chicago," so she went there immediately. Another time she thought she heard a mysterious voice say: "There is a way of preserving food without cooking it." Amanda knew absolutely nothing about jars and cans, but that didn't matter. The voice had spoken. So Amanda studied and experimented. In the end, Amanda found a way to pump the air out of a can before putting the food inside. This "vacuum process" kept it fresh. Next time you open a can of soup, listen for Amanda's mysterious voices.

Estimate how many marbles will fit in a can. Try it and see.

October

20

Jomo Kenyatta
1891, Kenya

Jomo's motto was *Harambee*—"Let's all pull together." It was a good choice for the man who became Prime Minister of Kenya. Jomo helped unify Kenyans who spoke different languages or lived far apart. He knew the nation would be better off if everyone could "pull together." When Jomo came to power, Kenya had just won a long struggle with Britain for its independence. Many Europeans and Asians weren't sure if they should stay in Kenya or go home. Jomo encouraged them to remain and "pull together" with native Kenyans. For his work, Jomo was called *Mzee*— "grand old man."

Make up a motto for yourself. Why did you choose it?

From *Birthday a Day*, published by GoodYearBooks. Copyright © 1996 Stephen Currie.

Alfred Nobel

1833, Sweden

Alfred left all his money to set up five prizes named after himself. Three of the five go to scientists. One is for a writer, and the fifth goes to a person who has worked for peace. Why peace? Alfred had invented dynamite. He thought his invention would end war. Battles would become so dangerous, he said, that people would have to stop fighting. Too many soldiers would die if dynamite were used. But Alfred was wrong. Besides helping to build roads and bridges, dynamite was used to make bombs. In fact, it made wars worse. The Nobel Peace Prize was Alfred's way of apologizing.

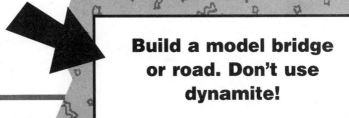

Build a model bridge or road. Don't use dynamite!

Sarah Bernhardt

1844, France

Sarah traveled a lot. Wherever she went, she brought her pets. That sounds perfectly reasonable, except that Sarah's pets were alligators, turtles, and monkeys—even a lion. But no one complained. Sarah was the most popular actress of her time. Even today, anyone who's very dramatic is called a "Sarah Bernhardt."

Sarah earned her fame. She put so much energy into her performances that she usually fainted once they were over. After she lost a leg, she kept right on acting. During her final illness, when she was almost eighty, Sarah turned her bedroom into a studio so she could star in a movie!

Make as many facial expressions as you can. Tell what feelings they represent.

From *Birthday a Day*, published by GoodYearBooks. Copyright © 1996 Stephen Currie.

October

23

Pele
1940, Brazil

Pele once shined shoes for a living. Later on, he trained to be a shoemaker. But we remember Pele for something else he did with shoes: kicking a soccer ball.

Pele might have been the best soccer player ever. He led the Brazilian national team to three World Cup titles. The first came when he was only seventeen. He was so good, people said the ball looked like it was attached to his feet by an invisible string. But then, Pele didn't need a real soccer ball to be a great player. When he was a boy, he couldn't afford to buy a ball. So he rolled up some socks and kicked them instead!

Besides socks, think of three other ways to make a ball. Draw them.

From *Birthday a Day*, published by GoodYearBooks. Copyright © 1996 Stephen Currie.

October 24

Sarah Josepha Hale
1788, New Hampshire

Sarah was always writing. She wrote stories, letters, and books. But her most famous work was a short poem about a girl named Mary, who had this little lamb . . .

As editor of a magazine, Sarah put lots of her own work in each issue. She shared her opinions about holidays (everyone should celebrate Thanksgiving), beards (men should shave them off), and recipes (would you eat "Lafayette Ducks with Snow-Balls"?). Sarah became an editor by accident. Her husband died without leaving her any money. But once she started, she didn't stop. She worked as an editor for nearly fifty years!

Plan your own magazine. What articles will you have?

From *Birthday a Day*, published by GoodYearBooks. Copyright © 1996 Stephen Currie.

October 25

Pablo Picasso
1881, Spain

Pablo was an artist. Many of his six thousand paintings were a little unusual. When he painted a face, it was likely to have four eyes, green hair, or an extra nose where an ear should be. Sometimes Pablo would paint several different views of the same face and stick them all on one body. Other times, Pablo might scatter pieces of a person into different parts of the picture. It helped that Pablo had amazing concentration. He could work for hours without changing position. "Don't you get tired?" a friend once asked him. "No," Pablo explained. "I leave my body outside."

Look at some of Pablo's work. Draw a picture that fits his style.

October

26

Mahalia Jackson
1911, Louisiana

A passage in the Bible tells people to "make a joyful noise unto the Lord." Mahalia certainly did!

Mahalia grew up in a deeply religious family. Her father did not allow his children to listen to music that wasn't about God. In fact, Mahalia did listen to jazz and opera at friends' houses. But like her father, she preferred to sing "gospel" music—songs with biblical themes. Many of her recordings sold over a million copies. Mahalia was encouraged to sing other styles, but she refused. "Gospel singing is a heart feeling," she said. "That's what I've got to sing if I'm going to sing at all."

List all the styles of music you can think of.

From *Birthday a Day*, published by GoodYearBooks. Copyright © 1996 Stephen Currie.

October

27

Isaac Merrit Singer

1811, New York

Sewing machines used to be pretty dreadful. They'd only sew a few stitches at a time, or the cloth would bunch up, or the threads would break. Then Isaac came along. He understood machinery. Looking carefully at all the other machines, Isaac combined all the ideas he could find that worked. Then he built his own model. It was the first machine that could actually sew. But Isaac didn't build it to make life easier for people. He said he did it "for the dimes." Selling his new machines gave him plenty. He needed them too. He had twenty-four children and a house with one hundred and fifteen rooms!

Look closely at your shirtsleeve. Estimate how many stitches are in it.

October

28

Kate Brandegee
1844, Tennessee

Kate and her husband had an unusual honeymoon. Right after getting married, they walked five hundred miles through California, collecting plants. For Kate, though, the trip was a blast. Kate was a botanist. She studied plants, and she loved them more than anything. Kate had considered studying insects or birds, but chose plants instead. She ran a plant museum and wrote magazine articles about rare plants. Her own collection at home had over seventy-five thousand different kinds! No wonder even her friends said that Kate was a terrible housekeeper.

Invent your own species of plant. Draw and describe it.

From *Birthday a Day*, published by GoodYearBooks. Copyright © 1996 Stephen Currie.

Harriet Powers

1837, Georgia

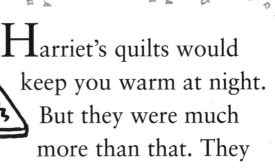

Harriet's quilts would keep you warm at night. But they were much more than that. They were works of art—and pieces of Harriet's life.

Harriet used her quilts to tell stories. First, she divided her quilt into sections. Then, she cut out figures from cloth. Next, Harriet sewed the cloth figures in place so each section told its own story. Some of these stories were based on events that had happened to Harriet. Others came from the Bible. No one knows how many quilts Harriet might have made during her lifetime. A hundred years later, only two survive.

Design your own story quilt. What stories will you tell?

Charles Atlas
1894, Italy

Charles could pull six cars at once. He bent metal spikes with his bare hands. But when he was twelve years old, he was so weak he could barely climb a flight of stairs.

What made the difference? Exercise. Grab one hand with the other and pull hard with both arms. Feel the muscles working in your back and shoulders? Charles thought up many exercises like this. Doing them every day, over many years, developed his chest, legs, stomach, and neck—even his fingers. Soon Charles was known as the strongest man on earth. Not bad for a boy who used to be a "98-pound weakling"!

Invent your own "Charles Atlas" exercise.

From *Birthday a Day*, published by GoodYearBooks. Copyright © 1996 Stephen Currie.

31

Daisy Low
1860, Georgia

Daisy was fifty years old and terribly bored. Then she heard about a man named Robert Baden-Powell, who had started the Boy Scouts. Daisy grew excited. She decided to start a similar program for girls. Daisy asked her friends to help her organize things. When they told her they didn't have time, Daisy wasn't discouraged. Instead, she pretended to misunderstand them. She'd smile and say "Oh, I'm so glad you can do it!" Usually they were too embarrassed to correct her. Daisy signed up dozens of "volunteers" that way. Before long, there were Girl Scout troops all across the world.

Write a skit showing how Daisy got her way.

November 1

Miriam Whitcher
1811, New York

No one appreciated Miriam while she was growing up. She used to draw perfectly wonderful cartoons of the adults she knew, but those adults never seemed to admire them. She also wrote funny poems about her classmates, but they didn't find the poems so amusing. As an adult, Miriam wrote books about silly people living in small towns. At a time when most women writers were only producing hymns and serious novels, Miriam made people laugh. Her books were very popular. Except among Miriam's neighbors, of course. They thought she was really writing about them.

> **Write a story or a poem that will make someone laugh.**

From *Birthday a Day*, published by GoodYearBooks. Copyright © 1996 Stephen Currie.

November 2

Marie Antoinette
1755, Austria

When Marie was born, people cheered and danced in the streets. When she became Queen of France, there was dancing again. But then things began to go wrong. Marie wore three fancy dresses each day and owned jewels worth millions of dollars. She had fine food, hundreds of servants, and a park all to herself.

The money came from taxes on the French people. They couldn't afford it. They could barely feed themselves. But Marie didn't care. Her attitude led to a revolution against the royal family. Marie's head was chopped off. And, once more, there was dancing in the streets.

Write a news report about some part of Marie's life.

November 3

The Earl of Sandwich
1718, England

John Montagu was the fourth Earl of a place called Sandwich. Though John was supposed to be making laws, he preferred to gamble. Since he wouldn't even stop gambling long enough to eat, his servants brought him platters of meat and cheese for dinner. Still, John wasn't happy. He needed both hands to cut and eat the food he was served. That used up precious gambling time! So he ordered the servants to put his food between two slices of bread. That way, he could eat with one hand while he gambled with the other. This new food caught on, and John's "sandwich" became famous.

Take a survey of people's favorite sandwiches. Make a graph.

From *Birthday a Day*, published by GoodYearBooks. Copyright © 1996 Stephen Currie.

Ruth Handler

1916, Colorado

Ruth and her husband ran a toy company. They got ideas for new toys by watching their children play. Ruth's daughter especially liked paper dolls. Her favorites were teenagers that came with fashionable clothes. She wanted a teenage doll to carry around and dress, but most toy companies only made baby dolls. So Ruth designed one herself. She marketed plenty of clothes for it too. Three years later, the Handlers issued a boy doll. They named the dolls after their children, Barbara and Kenneth. Stumped? Try their nicknames: "Ken" and "Barbie."

If a doll is a foot high, how long should its arm be? Explain why.

From *Birthday a Day*, published by GoodYearBooks. Copyright © 1996 Stephen Currie.

Ida Tarbell

1857, Pennsylvania

Oil. We use it every day: to heat houses, to make into gasoline, to stop bicycle gears from squeaking. In 1900, oil was a problem. One company controlled most of the U.S. supply. It could put other companies out of business if it wanted—and it did. It could raise prices whenever it liked. Customers had two choices: pay, or do without.

Ida was a reporter who was asked to study the oil business. She wrote an article about the unfair system. She got so interested, she wrote eighteen more! Ida's work helped get new laws passed that made companies less powerful.

Choose another important product. Make a list of ways it can be used.

From *Birthday a Day*, published by GoodYearBooks. Copyright © 1996 Stephen Currie.

John Philip Sousa
1854, *District of Columbia*

Ever seen a tuba? It's a big brass instrument with a bell that points straight up. Tubas sound great, but when it rains during a parade, it rains right into the bell. So John built a new tuba whose bell pointed to the side. Its name? A "sousaphone," of course.

For fifty years, John was a band leader. But he is best remembered for writing more than a hundred marches, including the famous "Stars and Stripes Forever." It didn't take much for John to write a new march. He wrote marches in honor of cities, cotton, even a newspaper. When he wrote his autobiography, he called it—what else?—*Marching Along.*

Draw a new musical instrument. Name it. What does it sound like?

7

Marie Curie
1867, Poland

Who says scientists need fancy equipment and huge labs? Marie won two Nobel Prizes working in a drafty old shed.

Marie suspected that a rock called "pitchblende" contained tiny bits of an unknown metal. For four years she worked to find it. There was amazingly little. Eight tons of pitchblende gave her less than a gram of her new metal. But just as she had predicted, it was there. Marie called her discovery "radium." Radium sends out rays a little like X rays. It is used today in treating cancer. Unfortunately, it also can be a poison. Over time, Marie's greatest discovery killed her.

Look at some rocks with a magnifying glass. Draw what you see.

From *Birthday a Day*, published by GoodYearBooks. Copyright © 1996 Stephen Currie.

Milton Bradley
1836, Maine

Milton's name appears on many board games. That's because Abraham Lincoln grew a beard.

In 1860, when Lincoln ran for President, Milton was a printer. Hoping to get rich, he printed up thousands of copies of Lincoln's photograph. He meant to sell them all. But he didn't sell a single one, because Lincoln had grown a beard, which completely changed his looks. Milton was practically broke. So when an inventor came to him with a potentially money-making idea for a board game, Milton agreed to print it. The game sold forty-five thousand copies the first year, and Milton was in the games business to stay!

Make your own board game. Write down the rules.

From *Birthday a Day*, published by GoodYearBooks. Copyright © 1996 Stephen Currie.

Benjamin Banneker
1731, Maryland

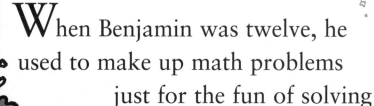

When Benjamin was twelve, he used to make up math problems just for the fun of solving them. A few years later, Benjamin saw a watch for the first time. He was fascinated, so he decided to build his own clock. It wasn't easy. He used his math skills to figure out how big the pieces would have to be. Then Benjamin drew up a plan and started to build. He carved each gear out of wood. One by one, he fit the pieces together. The whole process took months. But when he was done, Benjamin had the first clock ever built in America. Did it work? You bet. It kept perfect time for forty years!

Draw a clock. Show what you think might be inside.

From *Birthday a Day*, published by GoodYearBooks. Copyright © 1996 Stephen Currie.

Martin Luther
1483, Germany

Martin was a Catholic priest. He frequently disagreed with the leaders of his church, though. One day Martin got fed up. He wrote down his complaints—ninety-five of them!—and nailed the list to the door of his church, where anyone could see them. Martin's bosses were furious. They arrested Martin and tried to make him apologize. He wouldn't. "Here I stand," he said. "I can do no other." When they kicked him out of the church,

Martin started his own. Many people joined him. Because they were protesting, we call them "Protestants" today. Martin had changed the Christian religion forever.

Write a skit about what Martin did. Perform it.

From *Birthday a Day*, published by GoodYearBooks. Copyright © 1996 Stephen Currie.

Abigail Adams

1744, Massachusetts

Abigail was the wife of one president and the mother of another. She also wrote letters. Hundreds of letters. Thousands of letters. Even though Abigail had trouble with handwriting and spelling, she wrote to friends, relatives, and practically anyone else she'd ever met. Abigail wrote letters about everything. She wrote about her family's farm. She explained why all children should go to school. She gave her opinions on the big questions of the time. One of Abigail's letters even reminded her son to take "a cracker in his pocket" when he went to the Capitol to make laws for the country!

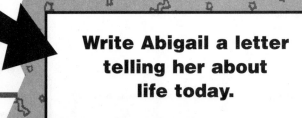

Write Abigail a letter telling her about life today.

From *Birthday a Day*, published by GoodYearBooks. Copyright © 1996 Stephen Currie.

November 12

Sun Yat-sen
1866, China

You've escaped from jail. For several weeks you've traveled only at night. Now you've come to a city where you might be safe. You're about to go into it when you see your name and face—on a "Wanted" poster. There's a huge reward too. What do you do?

If you were Yat-sen, you got out of that city right away. Yat-sen was trying to bring democracy to China. He spent a lot of time hiding. Even when he left the country, he wasn't safe. Once he was kidnapped in England! But Yat-sen didn't give up. In 1911, he became China's first president and got rid of emperors for good.

Design your own Wanted poster.

13

Augustine of Hippo
354, Algeria

Catholics who have done great things for their religion are sometimes made "saints" after their deaths. Augustine was a saint, but if you'd known him when he was a young man, you'd never have believed it. Back then, Augustine wasn't a godly person at all. For years, he ignored Catholic teachings. He used to pray that God would make him a good man— "but not yet." When Augustine did become a Christian, he changed his life completely. He became bishop of a town called Hippo, and he wrote many books about religion. Though Augustine died more than fifteen hundred years ago, some of his books are still read today.

What books do you think will be read 1500 years from now? Why?

From *Birthday a Day*, published by GoodYearBooks. Copyright © 1996 Stephen Currie.

Claude Monet

1840, France

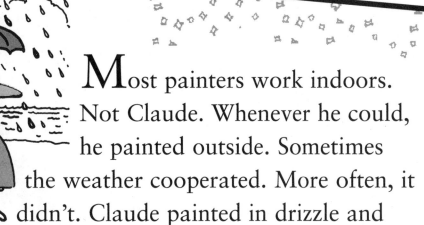

Most painters work indoors. Not Claude. Whenever he could, he painted outside. Sometimes the weather cooperated. More often, it didn't. Claude painted in drizzle and fog. When he got close to the ocean, he got splashed by waves. Once in a while he even had to tie his canvas onto the easel, so the paintings wouldn't blow away. But Claude didn't mind. He was fascinated by sunlight and the way it reflected off water at different times of day. Nasty weather could actually make his paintings more interesting. Did Claude die of pneumonia at age twenty-five? Nope. He lived into his eighties!

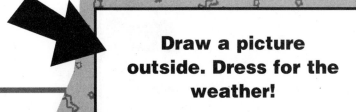

Draw a picture outside. Dress for the weather!

November 15

Georgia O'Keeffe
1887, *Wisconsin*

W hen Georgia was a very little girl, she saw a quilt with vivid red and black patterns. Ever afterwards, she remembered the way the light struck the quilt and made the colors even richer. Georgia liked sewing and building as a child. But she was most interested in art, so she became a painter. Most of Georgia's pictures showed just one object. She painted brilliant close-ups of flowers, and brownish-gray animal skulls lying in the desert. Georgia's favorite color combination was deep red against pure black. Sound familiar? It should. It was just what she'd seen on that quilt.

Paint a picture that Georgia would appreciate.

From *Birthday a Day*, published by GoodYearBooks. Copyright © 1996 Stephen Currie.

November 16

Chinua Achebe
1930, Nigeria

Have you ever read a book and said "I can do better than that!"? So did Chinua. At age eighteen, Chinua read a novel about Africa. Dozens of people read the book and said "How wonderful!" Chinua read it and said "How stupid!" He saw that the author knew nothing about Africa. So he started writing his own stories. Chinua's books described how hard it was for Africans and Europeans to understand each other. His most famous novel, *Things Fall Apart*, was translated into forty-five languages. He even won the Wrong prize for it. A prize in honor of a woman named Margaret Wrong, that is!

List all the languages you can. Can you think of forty-five?

November 17

August Mobius
1790, Germany

August studied "barycentric calculus" and "homogeneous coordinates." But his most famous mathematical discovery was a piece of paper. First he cut a long, narrow strip. He twisted it once and glued the ends together into a loop. The twisted loop looked perfectly normal, but it wasn't. It had only one side and one edge. The inside was the outside. To prove it, make one yourself. Try to color the inside of the loop red and the outside blue. After you put red around the inside, you'll keep going around the outside too. There's no room for blue! In August's honor, we call this amazing loop a Mobius strip.

Make a Mobius strip. Do some experiments with it.

From *Birthday a Day*, published by GoodYearBooks. Copyright © 1996 Stephen Currie.

November
18

Wilma Mankiller
1945, Oklahoma

Like many Americans, Wilma moved to California when she was a young woman. She got a job, she went to college, she raised her children. But unlike most people who went to California, she didn't stay. Instead, she headed back home—to become chief of the Cherokee Nation!

Being chief wasn't easy. Half of the Cherokee didn't have jobs. Others had little education. Wilma helped start new businesses and schools. But she had a bigger goal: to pull the community together. "I want to be remembered," she said, "as the person who helped us restore faith in ourselves."

List three ways you could help pull your own community together.

George Rogers Clark

1752, Virginia

The Northwest. Oregon, Idaho, and Washington, right? Wrong. In George's day, the Northwest meant states like Illinois and Michigan. During the Revolution, George was in charge of keeping the British out of the "Northwest." It was a tough job. At one point George's army had just 175 men. In the middle of winter, they had to wade across freezing rivers. Sometimes they ran out of food. But George held onto most of the territory. And when the war was over, the U.S. got to keep it all. If it hadn't been for George, a trip to Ohio today might be a trip to a foreign country!

Copy the shape of the U.S. Shade in the "old" and "new" Northwests.

From *Birthday a Day*, published by GoodYearBooks. Copyright © 1996 Stephen Currie.

November 20

Callie French
1861, Ohio

Callie and her husband owned an unusual theater. It had nine hundred and sixty seats, and it floated. Each year they took this "showboat" down rivers from Pittsburgh to New Orleans. When they came to a town, they put on a show. Callie sang, acted in plays, played the organ, and walked a tightrope. Because her husband had trouble steering boats, Callie took over that job too. She was the first woman pilot on the Mississippi River. In twenty years she never had an accident. When Callie retired, she took just one souvenir from her showboat: a bell made from the first silver dollars the Frenches had ever earned.

Design your own showboat.

21

Hetty Green
1835, Massachusetts

Poor Hetty. To save money on fuel, she ate cold oatmeal each morning. To save on clothes, she wore the same dress over and over. Hetty never threw out scraps of soap, and she lived in a tiny room—all to save money. Hetty liked saving money. She didn't really need to, though. She had almost a hundred million dollars!

Hetty had a head for business. She inherited about six million dollars. By investing it carefully, she became even richer. But she preferred to hoard her money. Hetty was called "The Witch of Wall Street" and "The World's Greatest Miser." Both nicknames seemed appropriate.

Think of four other ways of saving money. Write them down.

From *Birthday a Day*, published by GoodYearBooks. Copyright © 1996 Stephen Currie.

Billie Jean King

1943, California

Tennis was Billie Jean's sport. But it drove her crazy. Once she was kicked out of a tournament for wearing shorts instead of a dress. The best women players didn't earn as much money as men did. Fans weren't allowed to shout, the scoring system made no sense, and players had to wear white. Besides working to change a few of the rules, Billie Jean also became one of the best players around. In 1967, she won three championships at a tournament called the U.S. Open. That was nothing new for Billie Jean, though. She'd just done the same thing at a tournament called Wimbledon!

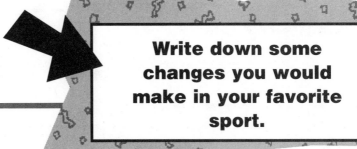

Write down some changes you would make in your favorite sport.

November 23

Billy the Kid
1859, New York

By the time Henry McCarty was fifteen, both his parents were dead. Without anyone to take care of him, Henry tried to be a tough guy. He drank, carried a gun, and gambled. He also started calling himself Billy. The problem was that Billy didn't look very tough. He was clumsy, and he didn't even own a pair of cowboy boots. When a man in a bar teased and bullied Billy, Billy shot and killed him. For four years he hid from the law, stealing cows and shooting people who got in his way. Billy was killed at the age of twenty-one—to be always remembered as Billy "the Kid."

Imagine you were traveling with Billy. What would it be like?

From *Birthday a Day*, published by GoodYearBooks. Copyright © 1996 Stephen Currie.

Scott Joplin
1868, Texas

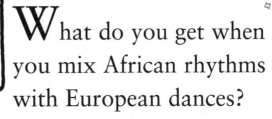

What do you get when you mix African rhythms with European dances?

You get ragtime music—and you get Scott. As a boy, Scott played pianos in houses where his mother worked as a maid. Later on, he studied music and composed his own pieces. Though Scott wrote marches, waltzes, and a couple of operas, he was best known for his bouncy "rags." One piece, the "Maple Leaf Rag," was the first sheet music ever to sell a million copies. When rags went out of fashion, Scott died in poverty. But you can still hear Scott's music today, played on piano, flute, trumpet, and even duck whistle!

Take a survey. What kinds of music do people like best? Make a graph.

Carry Nation
1846, Kentucky

Carry hated liquor. Her husband had died from drinking too much of it, and she knew other men who spent all their money on whiskey and rum. She decided to stop them. So she brought rocks into bars and threw them at the liquor bottles. Then she broke mirrors, knocked over tables, and tore the doors off refrigerators. Soon Carry found she could do even more damage with a hatchet. She was arrested often, of course. To pay her fines, she gave talks across the country. She sold souvenir hatchets too. Bar owners fought back, but in vain. Most bars simply shut down whenever Carry came to town!

Draw before and after pictures of a bar like one that Carry might have damaged.

From *Birthday a Day*, published by GoodYearBooks. Copyright © 1996 Stephen Currie.

November
26

Major Taylor
1878, *Indiana*

Major called himself "The Fastest Bicycle Rider in the World." For a long time, he was. He won most of the races he entered, and he set all kinds of records. But Major's toughest race came when he was just seventeen. The object was to ride around a track as many times as he could in six days. It was pure misery. Major would ride for eight hours, then sleep for one. During rest stops, he'd eat two fried chickens and four pounds of meat. It was barely enough to keep him going. In all, Major rode 1,732 miles. That's about the distance between Miami and Minneapolis. Where did he finish? Second.

Think about how a bicycle works. Write an explanation.

27

Fanny Kemble
1809, England

When Fanny was twenty-two, she toured the United States as an actress. Fanny played Juliet. Her father, who was fifty-seven, played Romeo. Fanny married an American, who took her to Georgia to live for a year. Fanny was appalled to find that her new husband owned slaves—and even more upset that he didn't see anything wrong with it. When they divorced, Fanny returned to England, where she published a diary of her year in the South. During the Civil War, the British were thinking of helping the Confederates. Fanny's book helped convince them not to.

Name three qualities an actress should have. Why are they important?

From *Birthday a Day*, published by GoodYearBooks. Copyright © 1996 Stephen Currie.

November

28

Allen Wright
1825, Mississippi

GREETINGS FROM OKLAHUMMA

It used to be called "Indian Territory." Now it's a state. Which one? Well, in the Choctaw Indian language, the word "okla" means "people." As for the word "humma," that's how you say "red." "Oklahumma" would be a way to say "red people." Spell it "Oklahoma," and you've got it.

"Oklahoma" was Allen's suggestion. Allen was a Choctaw leader who was very good at languages. If you wanted to know what a Choctaw word meant, he was the one to ask. He translated laws and poems between Choctaw and English. Allen also wrote *Chahta Leksikon*, the first Choctaw-English dictionary!

Make up a story about how a state got its name. Then find the *real story*.

Louisa May Alcott

1832, Pennsylvania

Louisa's stories won her fame and fortune. Unfortunately, she only wanted the fortune.

Louisa wrote quickly and almost never revised her work. Of her 275 books, the most famous was called *Little Women*. It was the story of four sisters, who were based on Louisa's own family. *Little Women* was a best-seller from the start. Its fans loved the book so much, they wanted to celebrate the author too. But Louisa just wanted to be left alone. Once a town invited her to visit. They promised parades and speeches in her honor. "Will you come?" they asked. Louisa wrote back one word: "Never!"

Write a story. Base the characters on your own family.

From *Birthday a Day*, published by GoodYearBooks. Copyright © 1996 Stephen Currie.

Mark Twain

1835, Missouri

If you want to find Mark in an encyclopedia, you have to look up Samuel Clemens, instead. That was Mark's real name. Mark is best known for his stories of life along the Mississippi River. Two of his most famous characters were Huckleberry Finn, who floated down the river on a raft, and Tom Sawyer, who lived on the river's edge. Mark himself grew up near the river. He even spent four years piloting boats up and down the Mississippi. But when he wrote about Huck and Tom, Mark was nowhere near the river he knew so well. He was living in Connecticut, a thousand miles away!

Build Huck Finn's raft out of sticks and paper. Make it float.

1

Madame Tussaud
1761, France

Madame Marie Tussaud was a very unusual artist. While most sculptors use metal or stone, Marie used wax. She made life-sized models of famous people. If she could, she used their actual faces to mold the wax. Then Marie dressed the statues and put them in a museum. Her work was amazingly good. Visitors couldn't stop pinching the models, just to make sure they weren't alive. Children often gave candy to wax babies. As a joke, real people sometimes sneaked into the exhibits. If they stood very still, it was almost impossible to tell them from the statues!

Make a clay statue of a friend. See if people can guess who it is.

From *Birthday a Day*, published by GoodYearBooks. Copyright © 1996 Stephen Currie.

December 2

Georges Seurat
1859, France

If you look at one of Georges's paintings from a distance, it looks perfectly normal: people in the park, a boat, some flowers. But if you look closely, all you see is dots. That's right. Georges's paintings were made up of thousands and thousands of tiny dots, each a different color from the one next to it. Yet they all fit together to make a beautiful painting. This technique is called "pointillism," and Georges invented it.

Georges spent two years on one of his biggest pictures. And that doesn't count two hundred sketches he'd made before he even started to paint!

Make your own pointillist picture with markers. Keep it small!

December

3

Barbara Fritchie

1766, Pennsylvania

Barbara was a heroine. Or was she?

During the Civil War, the Confederate Army marched into the Maryland town where Barbara lived. Only one Union flag was flying. When the commander ordered it taken down, a very old woman stuck her head out the window and dared the soldiers to shoot her instead. They didn't, and the flag stayed up. According to a poem written a little later, Barbara was this heroic woman. Her house was even made into a museum. But she wasn't the one. The real heroine was a woman named Mary Quantrell, instead. Oh well. Even poets make mistakes!

Act out what happened that day.

From *Birthday a Day*, published by GoodYearBooks. Copyright © 1996 Stephen Currie.

December

4

Chester Greenwood
1858, Maine

Chester liked to spend time outside with other kids. Unfortunately, during the winter his ears got terribly cold. Hats didn't help much. Then, as a teenager, Chester got an idea. He twisted a piece of wire so there was a circle at each end. Next, he asked his grandmother to sew furry cloth over the circles. He put the wire over his head, and presto! Chester had invented earmuffs. All his friends wanted them, too, so Chester built machines to produce them more quickly. He went on to invent an umbrella holder, a folding bed, even a doughnut hook. And it all started with cold ears.

Measure over a friend's head from ear to ear. How far is it?

From *Birthday a Day*, published by GoodYearBooks. Copyright © 1996 Stephen Currie.

December

5

Delia Akeley
1875, Wisconsin

Four times Delia went on an expedition to Africa. Each time she brought back something new: a bird she'd discovered, a new kind of antelope, a lion she had shot for a museum. But most of all, Delia enjoyed Africa for the people who lived there. Once she spent fourteen months living in African villages, getting to know the people and their ways. Delia's husband was also an explorer. But he had all kinds of trouble. He kept getting sick. He was even attacked by an elephant; luckily, Delia saved him. No wonder she always said that women were better explorers than men!

Was Delia right? Tell why you agree or disagree with her.

From *Birthday a Day*, published by GoodYearBooks. Copyright © 1996 Stephen Currie.

J. Eberhard Faber

1822, Germany

If Eberhard's name sounds familiar, check your pencils. One of them just might be his. Eberhard's family owned a pencil factory in Germany. As a young man, Eberhard came to the U.S. He opened a store and sold pencils, rubber bands, and writing supplies. Then Eberhard opened his own factory, which he named after himself. It was the first pencil factory ever built in the U.S., and it's still making "Eberhard Faber" pencils today. But Eberhard didn't just make pencils. He changed them forever. How? He was the first person to make pencils with erasers on the end!

Go on a pencil hunt. How many with Eberhard's name can you find?

December 7

Richard Sears
1863, Minnesota

One of the biggest companies in America got its start because no one came to the Lost and Found.

Richard worked at a train station. One day, somebody left a box of watches on the platform. They were never claimed, so Richard sold them himself. With the money, he bought more watches, and sold them too. Next, Richard went into business with a watchmaker named Alvah Roebuck. Alvah did the building, Richard the selling. At first, their catalog only offered watches. As they made more money, they sold other products too. And Sears, Roebuck, Incorporated, was born.

Write your own catalog page. What will you sell?

From *Birthday a Day*, published by GoodYearBooks. Copyright © 1996 Stephen Currie.

December

8

James Thurber
1894, Ohio

James was a writer. His stories were simple and funny. He wrote about his aunt, who kept all the lights turned off so electricity wouldn't leak out. He wrote about his dog, who ate at the table because it bit people who tried to feed it on the floor. James also drew cartoons, even though he wasn't a good artist. He used as few pencil strokes as possible, and he never shaded things in properly. James wanted to learn to draw, but the editors who bought his cartoons stopped him. Bad drawing was what made his cartoons funny, they said. If he ever became good, he'd be terrible!

Draw a cartoon using as few pencil strokes as you can.

Emmett Kelly

1898, Kansas

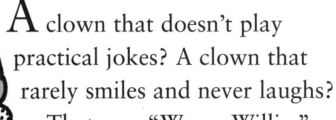

A clown that doesn't play practical jokes? A clown that rarely smiles and never laughs? That was "Weary Willie," Emmett's great creation. Emmett believed that a sad-faced circus clown could be funnier than a grinning one. Audiences felt bad for Weary Willie. He had no luck at all. He chased a spotlight around the ring without ever catching up. He even tried to crack peanuts with a sledgehammer. But feeling sorry didn't keep people from laughing. As for Emmett, he was quite happy being Willie. He once said he would rather be a clown than live in a palace, and he certainly got his wish.

See if you can make an audience laugh without ever smiling yourself.

From *Birthday a Day*, published by GoodYearBooks. Copyright © 1996 Stephen Currie.

Emily Dickinson
1830, Massachusetts

Most of Emily's neighbors would wonder why she was in this book. They didn't think she was great, just peculiar. For twenty years, Emily scarcely left her house. Most of the time she didn't come downstairs even when friends came to visit, and she only wore white. A few people knew she liked to write poems, but during her whole lifetime, she only published seven. Then Emily died, and seventeen hundred more poems were found. She had kept them a secret from nearly everyone. Now Emily is called one of the greatest American poets ever. Wouldn't her neighbors be surprised!

Emily wrote "The brain is wider than the sky." Was she right or wrong? Why?

From *Birthday a Day*, published by GoodYearBooks. Copyright © 1996 Stephen Currie.

Harriet Adams

1892, New Jersey

Harriet died of a heart attack while watching *The Wizard of Oz* on TV. She was nearly ninety years old. It was a good show for Harriet to be watching, though, because Harriet had always been involved in children's stories. If you've read the Nancy Drew books, you might know that they were written by Carolyn Keene. Actually, "Carolyn Keene" did not exist. Harriet edited the series, plotted most of the books, and wrote some of them herself. Harriet also wrote or planned books about the Hardy Boys, the Bobbsey Twins, and Tom Swift. In all, she was responsible for about twelve hundred books!

> **Make up a plot for a mystery story. Trade with a friend and write the words.**

From *Birthday a Day*, published by GoodYearBooks. Copyright © 1996 Stephen Currie.

Harry Warner

1881, Poland

Harry and his brothers started with a pig. Two years later, they added a duck. Next, they brought in a rabbit. No, it wasn't a zoo. It was a movie studio, and the animals were named Porky, Daffy, and Bugs.

For many years, the Warners made movies. They started their own film company, but they kept going broke. Since they had nothing left to lose, they tried something new—a movie with sound, called a "talkie." Many people said it couldn't be done. They were wrong. Others said no one would want to see it. They were wrong too. And the Warner brothers laughed all the way to the bank.

Make up three cartoon animals of your own.

Belle da Costa Greene

1883, Virginia

Belle's family wasn't very wealthy, so she loved working for J. P. Morgan. J. P. was one of the richest men on Earth. He had his own private library full of old and rare books. Belle had been hired to run it. She organized the books he had and bought many more with his money. That meant traveling. Next to rare books, Belle loved traveling best. She got to stay in fine hotels and wear fancy dresses. J. P. always paid the bills. Some of the books she bought for the library were hundreds of years old. By the time J. P. died, Belle had made the library so good it was opened to the public.

Ask people what their favorite book is. Make a graph.

From *Birthday a Day*, published by GoodYearBooks. Copyright © 1996 Stephen Currie.

December 14

Margaret Chase Smith
1897, Maine

Colleges often give "honorary" degrees to great people. Margaret had honorary degrees from thirty-six different colleges. Pretty good, considering she never went to college herself!

Margaret taught school, cut hair, and worked for a telephone company. But she didn't become famous until her husband died. He was a Congressman. Margaret filled out the rest of his term. Then she ran in the next election. She won. In fact, she got more votes than her husband ever had. In a time when women didn't usually hold office, Margaret served in Congress for more than three decades.

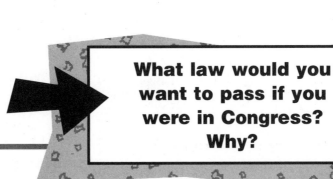

What law would you want to pass if you were in Congress? Why?

December
15

Ludwig Zamenhof
1859, Poland

Lernu la interlingvon Esperanto!

Everywhere he looked, Ludwig saw people who didn't get along. He knew what the problem was. Too many people couldn't understand each other's languages. So Ludwig invented a language of his own—Esperanto. He hoped all of Europe would soon be speaking it. Esperanto was easy to learn. Each letter stood for only one sound. Most of the words were already in European languages. Esperanto never caught on the way Ludwig hoped, but millions of people have learned it anyway. And that first sentence? It means "Learn the language Esperanto!"

Make up your own language. Write a few words in it.

Margaret Mead

1901, Pennsylvania

W hen Margaret was seven years old, her mother asked her to watch some younger children and write down what they did. Years later, Margaret did that full time. She was an anthropologist—a person who studies the way other people live. Margaret was especially interested in how children grew up in different societies. She visited countries across the globe. In each place, she talked to children and compared their experiences. She found lots of differences. But Margaret's information was not always right. Children around the world may be more alike than Margaret ever suspected!

Watch some younger children and write down what they do.

17

Deborah Sampson
1760, Massachusetts

Robert Shurtleff was a tall, strong soldier during the Revolution. He had plenty of friends, and he fought hard. But Robert had a secret. He was really Deborah—a woman. For a whole year, Deborah pretended to be a man. She wore the same clothes as the other soldiers. She bathed by herself, late at night. Even when she was wounded, no one caught on. Then Deborah got very sick. Though the doctor found her secret, he didn't tell anyone until the end of the war. In the meantime, Deborah went back to the army. Years later when she died, the names "Deborah" and "Robert" were both carved on her tombstone.

Name three qualities a soldier needs to have. Explain why you think so.

From *Birthday a Day*, published by GoodYearBooks. Copyright © 1996 Stephen Currie.

December

18

Steven Spielberg
1947, Ohio

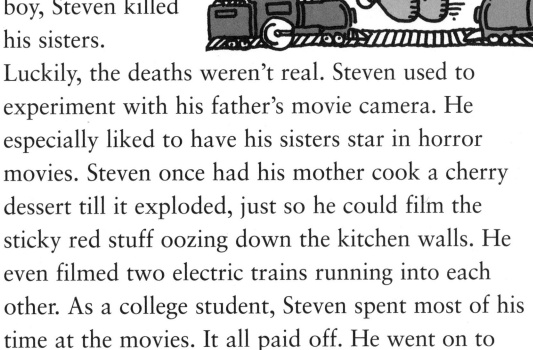

When he was a boy, Steven killed his sisters. Luckily, the deaths weren't real. Steven used to experiment with his father's movie camera. He especially liked to have his sisters star in horror movies. Steven once had his mother cook a cherry dessert till it exploded, just so he could film the sticky red stuff oozing down the kitchen walls. He even filmed two electric trains running into each other. As a college student, Steven spent most of his time at the movies. It all paid off. He went on to make movies like *E. T.*, *Jaws*, and *Raiders of the Lost Ark*—none of which starred his sisters.

Take a survey of people's favorite movies. Make a graph.

Cicely Tyson
1939, New York

What age would you like to be?

Whatever age you chose, Cicely could act it. In one movie role, she played a woman who lived to be one hundred and ten years old. Cicely had to look and act young to portray the woman when she was a teenager. She also had to play the woman at a hundred and ten—and several other ages in between. Some days it took six hours just to get Cicely's makeup on. Then she had to act for another six hours. Cicely had been a secretary and a model, but became an actress because she found those other jobs boring. One thing was for sure: with roles like that, Cicely never found acting to be dull!

Act out different ages. Let someone guess how old you are each time.

From *Birthday a Day*, published by GoodYearBooks. Copyright © 1996 Stephen Currie.

Lydia Hasbrouck
1827, New York

In Lydia's time, fashionable ladies wore huge skirts in the shape of hoops. Their dresses were covered with bows, laces, and little puffs. Of course, people who wore hoop skirts had trouble moving around. Lydia refused to wear them. Wanting to be comfortable, she wore an outfit called "bloomers"—a short skirt over loose pants. Bloomers probably don't sound very odd to you. But then, you weren't born in 1827. Lydia was told that bloomers were shocking and ugly. She was even kicked out of school for wearing them. From then on, Lydia fought so that women could wear sensible clothes.

Imagine you're wearing a hoop skirt. Take a walk. Don't bump into things!

December 21

Laura Bridgman
1829, New Hampshire

When Laura was two, she caught scarlet fever. It destroyed her sight and hearing, and it damaged her senses of taste and smell. But it didn't stop her. At age seven, Laura went to a special school. To teach her to communicate, teachers gave her metal letters that spelled out words like "KNIFE" or "CUP." Then they trained her to match the letters with real knives and cups. Laura did it easily, as if it were a game. Suddenly, one day she realized that the letters named the object. Soon she knew hundreds of words. Not only did Laura learn to read and write; she even taught blind students how to sew!

Make a domino tower with your eyes shut.

From *Birthday a Day*, published by GoodYearBooks. Copyright © 1996 Stephen Currie.

James Oglethorpe
1696, England

People who owe money are called "debtors." In James's time, debtors who couldn't pay what they owed were sent to jail. James helped make the laws in England, and he thought this was pretty stupid. He wondered how debtors could pay their debts if they were in prison. He couldn't get the law changed, so he did the next best thing. He started a new colony in America. The people he sent over were poor. Many were debtors. James hoped to give them a better life, and he did. As for the colony, he named it after his king, George the Second. And that's how Georgia got its start.

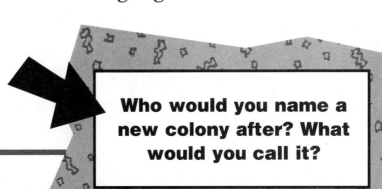

Who would you name a new colony after? What would you call it?

December

23

Madame Walker

1867, Louisiana

"Madame" Sarah Walker's hair was falling out, and she didn't know why. Then she dreamed about an old man mixing chemicals. He said they could get her hair back. When Sarah woke up, she bought the chemicals and tried them. They worked! "My hair was coming in faster than it had ever fallen out," she said later. Next, she tried her new formula on her friends. It made their hair even more beautiful, so Sarah bottled her formula and sold it. It might have been the dream, or it might have been good business sense. Whatever it was, it made Sarah the first African American woman millionaire.

Write down a dream you've had.

From *Birthday a Day*, published by GoodYearBooks. Copyright © 1996 Stephen Currie.

Kit Carson
1809, *Kentucky*

What color eyes did Kit have? No one knew for sure. After Kit died, some said brown, others blue. But everyone agreed that Kit's eyes had seen plenty of adventure. As a teenager, Kit ran away from home to live in the West. He got to know that part of the country very well. In fact, Kit often guided explorers and travelers. He climbed mountains in bitter cold and delivered messages across the desert heat. Kit hunted buffalo and moose too. For sixteen years, all the meat he ate came from animals he'd hunted. His eyes were good enough to see the target—and that was all that mattered!

Make a survey to find what eye color is most common among your friends.

Clara Barton
1821, Massachusetts

Clara was a nurse. She got her start when she was just eleven. Her older brother got very sick, and Clara helped nurse him back to health. It was good practice for her. During the Civil War, grateful soldiers called her "The Angel of the Battlefield." Later on, Clara started the American Red Cross. This group helped people who were victims of disasters like floods, fires, or war. Clara put all her energy into the Red Cross. Sometimes her friends told her she should stay behind a desk. But Clara wouldn't. For twenty-three years, she cooked soup and brought supplies to people in trouble.

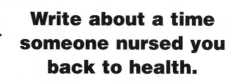

Write about a time someone nursed you back to health.

From *Birthday a Day*, published by GoodYearBooks. Copyright © 1996 Stephen Currie.

Susan Butcher

1954, Massachusetts

When she was growing up, Susan liked dogs and the outdoors. Then she discovered sled dog racing. It was a perfect fit. At age nineteen, Susan moved to Alaska. She trained dogs to run fast and follow commands. Once her team of dogs pulled a sled up the highest mountain in the U.S. Susan also competed in a race called the Iditarod. The Iditarod's course was more than a thousand miles long. The temperature could reach fifty below zero. Susan had to deal with angry moose, sick dogs, and winds of one hundred and forty miles an hour. Still, Susan always finished the race. She also won it three times!

Get some friends and act out a sled dog team with them.

December

27

Louis Pasteur
1822, France

PASTEUR

Louis knew what caused disease, but most people didn't believe him. No wonder. His theory was really bizarre. Louis imagined tiny things called "germs." No one could see germs, but that didn't stop Louis. He said that germs flew through the air, too, when everyone knew that only birds, bats, and balloons could fly. Louis even thought you could stop food from spoiling if you heated it and kept it away from air. He called it "pasteurization." Back in the 1800s, Louis's theory sounded crazy. But it was right. His ideas help us fight sickness—and keep us from getting sick in the first place.

Get permission to leave some food out. Watch it carefully. Record what you see.

From *Birthday a Day*, published by GoodYearBooks. Copyright © 1996 Stephen Currie.

Eliza Pinckney
1722, Antigua

When Eliza was seventeen, her parents put her in charge of a farm in South Carolina. She decided to grow rice and a plant called "indigo." Indigo was used to make dye. Eliza knew that cloth makers in England needed it. No one in South Carolina had ever had much luck planting indigo. But Eliza experimented, and she figured out a way to make it grow. Then she told her neighbors how to do it. For the next thirty years, indigo was South Carolina's main product. If you've ever seen indigo in a rainbow, you have an idea what color dye indigo made: different shades of blue.

Mix colors and keep records of what you get.

Charles Goodyear

1800, Connecticut

Rubber was useful stuff, but it had its problems. It stuck together in the heat and broke apart in the cold. Charles tried to find a way to make rubber easier to use. He mixed it with metal, alcohol, paint remover, and anything else he could find. One day, by accident, he dropped a mixture of rubber and sulphur on a hot stove. The intense heat did the trick. It made the rubber soft, dry, and flexible. Did Charles make a fortune? Nope. Perfecting the recipe took years. To stay alive, Charles sold his property—even his children's schoolbooks! He died a famous inventor, but $200,000 in debt.

Freeze a rubber ball or an eraser. Does it change? How?

From *Birthday a Day*, published by GoodYearBooks. Copyright © 1996 Stephen Currie.

Rudyard Kipling

1865, India

Rudyard was a writer who got ideas everywhere. Once he watched a cobra fighting a mongoose. That became his famous story "Rikki-Tikki-Tavi." Another time, Rudyard heard about a boy who might have been raised by wolves. That became *The Jungle Book*. But another book began much closer to home. Rudyard used to tell his daughter Josephine the same stories every night. If he changed them, even a little, she complained. She wanted the stories "just so"—just right—and made him go back and fix his mistakes. When he turned them into a book, he called them *The Just So Stories*.

Write a "Just So" story telling how something in nature began.

Odetta
1930, Alabama

Odetta's full name was a little longer: Odetta Holmes Felious Gordon Sheed Minter, to be exact. Odetta was a singer who had an incredibly powerful voice. One of her favorite songs was about a wall that tumbled down at the sound of a trumpet. Many listeners said her voice could have knocked down that wall all by itself!

Odetta also played the guitar. She learned how when she was already an adult. Often she made up her own way of playing chords. Her first guitar was secondhand, but Odetta didn't mind. She kept it for years. She even gave it a name: "Baby."

What's your favorite musical instrument? Explain why.

From *Birthday a Day*, published by GoodYearBooks. Copyright © 1996 Stephen Currie.

Pronunciations

JANUARY

1
2 LITE-zel
3 Loo-CREE-shuh
4 LOO-ee BRAY-ill
5 Jah-HAHN (second syllable rhymes with *Don*)
6
7 ZORE-uh
8 BULL-uhk
9 BY-ez
10
11 HAM-uhl-tuhn
12 I-ruh HAZE
13
14 SHWITE-zer
15
16 SIGZ-bee
17
18
19
20
21 LED-bell-ee
22 CORE-uh-guhn
23
24 TAWL-cheef
25 Core-a-SOHN ah-KEE-no
26 vahn TROP (rhymes with *drop*)
27 VOLF-gahng Ah-muh-DAY-us MOTE-sart
28 PAH-luhck
29 OH-pruh WIN-free
30
31

FEBRUARY

1 HYOOS
2 YAHSH-uh HI-fits
3
4
5 BELL
6 LEE-kee
7 ING-guhls WILE-der
8 JOOLZ VERN
9 LID-ee-uh PINK-um
10
11 AL-vuh ED-i-suhn
12
13
14 FARE-iss
15
16 BER-gun (hard g)
17 MARE-ee-uhn
18
19 Co-PER-nic-us
20 An-jel-EE-nuh GRIM-kee
21
22
23 doo-BOYS
24 VIL-helm
25 IB-uhn but-TOO-tuh
26 LEE-vie STROWSS
27
28
29 joh-ah-KEE-no ruh-SEE-nee

MARCH

1 bell-uh-FAHN-tay
2
3 KER-see
4 GARE-uht
5 Mer-KAY-ter
6 My-kel-AN-jel-o
7
8 GRAT-um
9 FISH-er
10
11 Mic-FARE-in
12
13 Suh-LAH-tay TOO-pooh
14 INE-stine
15
16 ROSE-en-thawl
17 GREEN-a-way
18
19
20 Mit-soo-MAH-suh AHN-noh
21 YO-hahn BAHCK (rhymes with *rock*)
22 Mar-SELL Mar-SO
23
24 Hoo-DEE-nee
25 GOOT-son BORG-lum
26
27
28
29
30 van GO
31 SAY-sar CHAH-vez

APRIL

1 BAHCK (sort of, as before)
2 HAHNTS
3 GOOD-all
4 MY-uh AN-jel-oh
5 mar-TEE-nez
6 BECK-werth
7
8 SONE-ya HEN-ee
9
10 OH-mar shuh-REEF
11
12 CLEER-ee
13
14
15 lee-uh-NAR-doh duh VIN-chee
16 kuh-REEM ahb-dool-juh-BAR
17
18 (rhymes with *arrow*)
19 SEE-borg
20
21 MYOOR
22
23
24
25 goo-LYEL-moh mar-COH-nee
26 PAY
27
28
29
30 GOUSS

MAY

1
2 uh-LIE-juh
3 GOLD-uh may-EER
4 LID-uhl
5

JUNE

6 duh-LAY-nee
7 AY-vuh pay-RONE
8 loo-CREE-shuh
9 BELL
10 uh-STARE
11 SAL-vuh-door DAH-lee
12 LEER
13
14 NICK-uhls
15 TEN-zing NOR-kay
16
17
18
19 MAL-cuhm
20
21
22 cuh-SAT
23 lin-NAY
24 GILL (hard G) - breth
25 dor-uh-THEE-uh LANG
26
27
28 dee-AHN
29
30 YOU-stiss
31

JUNE

1 ZHAHK (zh as in *treasure*) mar-KET
2 HED-duh
3
4
5 PAHN-choh VEE-ya
6 DAH-lie LAH-muh
7 AP-gar
8
9
10
11 Zhock Koo-STOW
12
13 AL-vuh-rez
14 STOH
15 ISS-uh
16 GOD-erd
17 ESH-er
18 an-uh-STAH-zee-uh ROH-muh-noff
19 ohng SAN soo chee
20 GOOLD
21
22 DIL-in-jer
23
24 guh-STAH-vus
25
26 DID-rik-suhn
27 an-twah-NET PARE-ee
28
29 GO-thuhlz
30 LEE-nuh

JULY

1 I-zuhk
2 (*TH* unvoiced)
3
4
5
6 FREE-duh KAH-loh
7 mah-ree-AH-no vuh-LAY-oh
8 RAF-ee
9 BOYT
10 muhk-LOUD buh-THOON

11
12
13 JOO-lee-us SEE-zer
14
15 van RINE
16
17 loo-EES moon-YOZE ree-VAY-ruh
18 hi-uh-COW-uh
19
20 REN-suh-leer
21 REE-no
22
23
24 BOH-luh-var
25 MAV-uh-rick
26
27
28 BEE-uh-trix
29
30
31

AUGUST

1
2 pee-AIRE lahn-FAHN (sort of)
3 uh-LIE-shuh
4 rah-OOL WAHL-uhn-berg
5
6 BUNCH
7 ES-ter
8
9 TRAV-erz
10
11
12
13
14
15 nuh-POH-lee-uhn BOH-nuh-part
16 yah-MAH-gah SOH-koh
17
18
19
20
21 BAY-see
22
23 PARE-ee
24
25
26 mahnt-GAHL-fee-er
27 tuh-REE-suh
28
29
30
31

SEPTEMBER

1 SAY-zhee oh-ZAH-wuh
2 lee-LEE-ooh-oh-kuh-LAH-nee
3
4 BER-nuhm
5
6
7
8
9 KER-nuhl
10
11
12 ah-nuh-GEE-toh (hard G)
   PARE-ee
13

14 I-vuhn PAV-lahv
15 YAHN maht-SELL-uh-ger (hard G)
16 NAH-dee-uh boo-lahn-ZHAY
17 mat-SOO-ee
18 GAR-boh
19
20
21
22 AS-ter
23 TARE-uhl
24
25 chen-LOONG (stressed vowel as in *book*)
26
27
28
29 LEK (close enough) vuh-LEH-suh
30 RIG-lee

OCTOBER

1
2 muh-HAHT-muh GAHN-dee
3
4 SAHN-chez
5 MY-uh
6 HAM-er
7 TOO-too
8
9
10
11 ROSE-uh-velt
12 PERL MES-tuh
13
14
15
16
17 EE-vuhl kuh-NEE-vuhl
18 WIN-tuhn mar-SEL-iss
19 thee-uh-DOH-zhuh
20 JOH-moh ken-YAH-tuh
21 no-BELL
22 BERN-hart
23 PAY-lay
24 JOH-suh-fuh
25 PAHB-loh pi-KAH-soh
26 muh-HAY-lee-uh
27 I-zuhk
28 BRAN-duh-jee
29
30
31 LOH

NOVEMBER

1 WICH-er
2 an-twa-NET
3
4
5 TAR-bell
6 SOO-suh
7 CURE-ee
8 BAN-uh-ker
9
10
11
12 SOON (oo as in *book*) yaht-SEN
13
14 moh-NAY
15
16 CHI-noo-ah ah-CHAY-bay
17 MOH-bee-us
18

19
20
21
22
23
24
25
26
27
28
29
30

DECEMBER

1 too-SOH
2 suh-RAH
3 FRICH-ee
4
5 DEE-lee-uh AKE-lee
6 FAY-ber
7
8
9
10
11
12
13 BELL duh COS-tuh GREEN
14
15 ZAH-men-hahf
16 MEED
17
18 SPEEL-berg
19 SIS-uh-lee
20 HAZ-brook
21 BRIDJ-muhn
22 OH-guhl-thorp
23
24
25
26
27 LOO-ee pas-TER
28 uh-LIE-zuh PINK-nee
29
30 RUD-yerd
31

Index